Soil and

Spirit

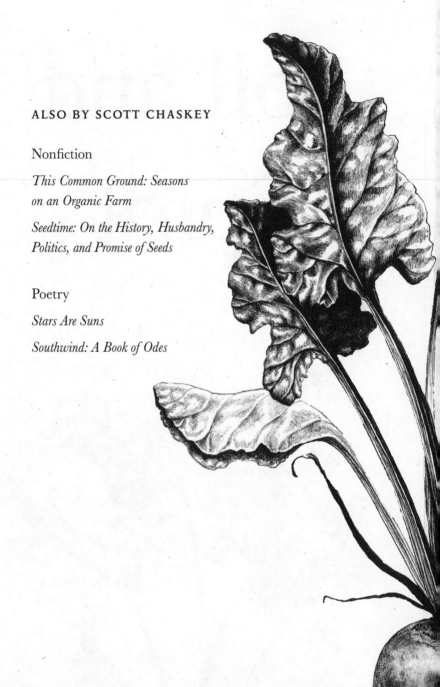

Soil and Spirit

Spirit

CULTIVATION

AND KINSHIP

IN THE WEB OF LIFE

SCOTT CHASKEY

MILKWEED EDITIONS

First paperback edition, published 2023 by Milkweed Editions
Printed in the United States of America
Cover design by Mary Austin Speaker
Cover illustration by Anne Løvenskjold
Interior illustrations by Liam Chaskey
Author photo by Lindsay Morris
23 24 25 26 27   5 4 3 2 1

978-1-63955-089-0

Library of Congress Cataloging-in-Publication Data

Names: Chaskey, Scott, author.
Title: Soil and spirit / Scott Chaskey.
Description: Minneapolis, Minnesota : Milkweed Editions, [2023] |
    Summary: ""Enlivened by decades of work in open fields washed by
    the salt spray of the Atlantic"-words that describe his prose as well
    as his vision of connectedness - Scott Chaskey has given us a book
    for our time: a seed of hope and regeneration in a time of widespread
    despair"-- Provided by publisher.
Identifiers: LCCN 2022037272 | ISBN 9781639550876 (hardback) |
    ISBN 9781639550883 (epub)
Subjects: LCSH: Chaskey, Scott. | Environmentalism. | Human
    ecology. | Nature poetry.
Classification: LCC GF47 .C46 2023 | DDC 304.2--dc23/
    eng20230422
LC record available at https://lccn.loc.gov/2022037272

Milkweed Editions is committed to ecological stewardship. We
strive to align our book production practices with this principle,
and to reduce the impact of our operations in the environment. We
are a member of the Green Press Initiative, a nonprofit coalition of
publishers, manufacturers, and authors working to protect the world's
endangered forests and conserve natural resources. *Soil and Spirit* was
printed on acid-free 100% postconsumer-waste paper by Sheridan
Saline.

For three generations of women:
My mother Mary, sisters Carol and Jane, my wife Megan, our
daughter Rowenna

And for my grandchildren, Aiden and Owen:
"Take from the palms of my hands
a little sun, a little honey . . ."
          Osip Mandelstam, Tristia

CONTENTS

A BREATH

Meadow man, house scholar,
   from field to chair
      I hear the deep choir of the anvil.
Iron and rust; irony, dust.

Then Nordic beat breaks to summer:
   willows wave, elderberry beads
      gift the cloud.
Dog rose shades the shore.

In a measure of rage
   I know the weightlessness of innocence.
      At dawn silken nursery tents
spin the field to song.

Sea air, violet betony stair
   shake the man to make
      of breath a mortal joy.

Soil and

Spirit

A GOLDEN-FLEDGED GROWTH

In the Forest of Arden, Shakespeare's Orlando hangs pages of odes on trees, a poetic variation on the signals that trees exchange underground through fungal hyphae and mycorrhizal social networks. Orlando's intention is romantic; that of the woodland plants—though we cannot be certain—less so, if equally ardent. We do know that we share with plants the same need and impulse to communicate, and recently we have been reawakened to our evolutionary friendship with other species, and to what Mary Evelyn Tucker calls the "ever-expanding dynamic circles of connectivity."

Stories are born when people come together in relationship, and stories connect us with other species that share our soils, our air, and our water. The challenges that confront us daily in the twenty-first century—familial, social, economic, political, environmental—can be overwhelming. And as we encounter what is reported as the greatest challenge humanity has collectively faced, climate disruption (the term Ralph Nader prefers, as do I), it is timely to revisit an ancient theme, an interspecies theme—our kinship with nature. In his wise and playful book *Mesquite,* my friend Gary Paul Nabhan, ethnobotanist and Franciscan brother, introduces the Mexican rancher Ivan Aguirre: "Part of our role here on this planet is to generate *riqueza.* How would you best say it in English? Richness? Abundance? Diversity? We are put here to observe the natural world and learn from its structure and its vigor."

Traditionally, in multiple cultures, academies of learning have been sited within a natural structure: a forest grove or arbor. In Ireland's ancient Brehon Law, a code of conduct, forest protection was of vital importance. Irish hedge schools, *scoileanna scairte*, were often situated in fields, in hedgerows, within a grove of trees. The prolific twentieth-century Indian writer and respected educator Rabindranath Tagore held classes under a canopy of leaves and branches. Of your two teachers, he advised, you will gain more wisdom from the trees.

My education most closely resembles an earthen fabric, woven together throughout decades of daily attention to soil structure (both loam and mycelium), and as a curious traveler exposed to diverse landscapes. I have learned through literature and in friendship with land. My teachers: poets, pine, oak, beech, stone, silt loam, the sharp-shinned hawk, and the windhover.

Years ago, I built a home on a steep hillside above the Cornish village of Mousehole, on the southwest coast of England, where I lived with my wife and first son for a decade. In a village built almost entirely of stone, originally of granite and slate and later concrete block—with a harbor wall dating from 1392—our house made of wood was an anomaly. I didn't have a clue how to build with stone—though eventually, out of necessity, I would dabble in the art of stone hedging, a common practice in a landscape of abundant granite and slate—so timber was the material of choice. After deconstructing (carefully) a homely pre-WWII bungalow made entirely of asbestos, we raised our timber framing on the original foundation, repairing and replacing blocks where needed, and we left the heart of the home, the hearth and chimney, intact, for a time open to the sky. Often at a loss of how to proceed, I was saved on countless days by the intuition, strength, and practical skills of my woodworking mate, Peter Perry, a member of the Men of the Trees (now known as the International Tree Foundation). Our labor with saws, chisels, and hammers was timed to the calls of jackdaws and gulls, and to the surge of the sea on granite just below. In the strong, straight flight of the shag (a cormorant) as she skimmed the surface of the bay, I perceived a way to act and to build day by day.

To stabilize our structure—a requirement of the local Penwith District Council—we engineered a truly handsome truss, known as a queen truss, made up of robust Douglas fir beams notched and bolted together, to bind the house in defense of the ferocious winds that seasonally assault the Penwith Peninsula.

I loved the symmetry of the wooden framing against the backdrop of the green, green hillside—fuchsia, bay, pittosporum, lush euonymus—and the granite retaining walls, and of course the wooden frame was an accurate, austere symbol of our significant labor; I was hesitant to enclose the space. But a roof and walls are basic necessities in a very wet climate, so I agreed to complete the job; we clad the structure in larch milled in northern Cornwall. Before we erected the interior walls, in a gesture reminiscent of early New England housebuilders who often placed a coin in the space between inside and outside, I tacked sheets of poems to the fir framing. Perhaps one day

a few fragments I wrote will survive, lines that resonate
with the wild of Penwith:

> The cliff breast shifts
> under weight of water.
> Near, bare sea vowels
> foam on stone.

Should the words be lost, the melody of creation lingers in
the coastal air.

When the great Northumbrian poet Basil Bunting,
whom you will meet in this book, was badgered to explain
the pattern, or beyond that, the meaning of his acclaimed
long poem *Briggflatts*, he drew a series of mountain peaks
that looked something like this:

His graphic explanation is enigmatic, but also leads
me deeper into the music of his poem, so I offer here my
best effort to map the journey I have been moved to write:

(A clue: the symbols all refer to natural forms.)

Throughout thirty years of farming on the South
Fork of Long Island, New York, my travels have led

me to return to the rugged Cornish Penwith Peninsula, where I first learned to cultivate plants, to a pueblo in New Mexico, to the southern coast of Maine, to an international gathering of community farming activists in China, and in memory to the west coast of Ireland. The thread that binds the story I have to tell is linked to an aspect of the mythic tale of the golden bough. This "golden-fledged growth," a scion of an oak, serves as talisman and key for the journey. Should the traveler be allowed to free a branch from the tree, another golden bough will sprout in its place, and thus another traveler will chance to pluck a living symbol of our symbiotic relationship with fecund, numinous, endangered nature. This book, through stories of people, plants, and place, explores that relationship.

The Japanese poet Matsuo Bashō, known as nature's pilgrim, saw in the movements of sun and moon across the sky a metaphor for a journey: "years coming or going wanderers too . . . each day is a journey and the journey itself home." We ourselves are whirling, day by day, within "circles of connectivity." What you will read in this book is the pulse of the bough when plucked, the pulse of the poems within the wall, the beat of the cormorant's wings in flight just above the sea surface, the salt spray tossing to touch the bird's wings . . . all part of the "miraculous that comes so close . . . wild in our breast for centuries."

Chapter 1

INEXHAUSTIBLE WAYS OF SEEING

It was, of course, the unseen world that interested her, but only as it lived in the world's details, most especially when it revealed itself in visible words.

—GIOIA TIMPANELLI, *SOMETIMES THE SOUL*

The rat, the mouse, the fox, the rabbet; watch the roots, the lion, the tyger, the horse, the elephant watch the fruits.

—WILLIAM BLAKE, "PROVERBS OF HELL,"

THE MARRIAGE OF HEAVEN AND HELL

As the beechnuts ripen, and the irresolute cold that is the hint of winter comes, starlings and grackles arrive in these island woods, in a cloud of wings. The sound is symphonic: hundreds or thousands of husks and nuts strike the roof and ground and the macadam driveway to supply the percussion; the birds, either the smaller starlings or the larger grackles with bright-yellow eyes, hundreds of them, supply the melody. Actually, the sound that arrives with the feeding birds is more chaotic than melodic, and it signals an alteration of time, a change of seasons. As a signal or a message, the birds could not be more effective—inside, at my desk, there is no avoiding the frenzied music; I am surrounded by it, within the shop, within the woods, under the canopy of the great American beech. Because of the way the tree hugs this wooden farm shop in the woods, it is safe to say that we share the experience, though certainly we sense it differently. The beech gives sustenance to starlings and grackles—the Latin name for beech, *Fagus*, is derived from the Greek *phagein*, "to eat"—I am but a grateful witness.

The story is told that Deborah Light's husband planned to build a garage to house his sizable boat. I am unsure why he chose this particular site—a steep sloping terrain within a thick woodland—but it was not far from the existing house. Deborah gave her permission on the condition that this fine specimen of *Fagus grandifolia* remain untouched. She was a conservationist, and she practiced what she believed in. She believed in the tree, and because of her eventual gift of this land to my employer, a conservation land trust, I too have formed a bond with this beech. For those who may have forgotten, a delightful Winnie-the-Pooh character also formed a close bond with a beech. *Pooh and Piglet Go Hunting* begins: "The Piglet lived in a very grand house in the middle of a beech-tree, and the beech-tree was in the middle of the Forest, and the Piglet lived in the middle of the house."

I have heard that beech trees do not like to have their roots restricted. Whether the architect or the builders of this structure were aware of this or not, they constructed the foundation to allow some wiggle room for the tree's roots. The beech stands at the entrance to the building, and fifty years after the first concrete block was placed, the beech and the building are now joined. There once was space to place and nail the fascia board that decorates the eave, but now the very alive trunk of the beech is wedded to common construction pine. Naturally, we have pruned the lower branches, though the upper branches, given the strength and resilience of beechwood, reach out and beyond the roof in every direction.

The bark of beech is very thin and smooth— throughout the life of the tree—and this characteristic has led people to compare beech bark to an elephant's skin. I prefer to picture the branches of beech as the long limbs of some mythical figure, part of a creation story perhaps, a figure with human and arboreal qualities equally balanced. The tree is beautiful in every season. Beech twigs are scaled and purplish-brown in winter, and the brown buds swell and elongate in April before leaf burst. Male catkins and the first leaves, a most delicate green, emerge together in May. Female catkins soon join the show, and each flower is wrapped with purple bracts. By midsummer the leaves have darkened and the fruits are covered with short swirling bristles. In fall, when the fruit is ripe, the husk opens to reveal (commonly) two triangular seeds, the prize that awaits the starlings. Though I admire the elegance and grace of the body of beech—twig and branch and bristled fruit—I am reminded by the German forester Peter Wohlleben that this living specimen is supported by what he calls "life's lower story." Wohlleben, steward and careful observer of a beech forest in Hümmel,

Germany, who recently made popular the concept of the "wood wide web," notes that one half of the biomass of a forest is unseen, underground.

For centuries, beech bark was used by scribes for writing tablets. Sheets of bark tied together became some of our first books; the Anglo-Saxon *bec* and German *boche*, root words for the beech tree, are similar to words meaning "book." The ancient Celts, before the invention of letters, created an alphabet using symbols of trees—each tree in essence a letter. The English poet Robert Graves (author of *The White Goddess*) reports that for the Druids *beech* was a synonym for *literature*. Having spent thirty years, on a near-daily basis, upstairs in a wooden structure under the canopy of one particular beech tree—planning the rotations of fields, ordering seeds and supplies, watching the weather, but always writing, poetic stanzas or pages to piece together a book—I believe in the synonym. The wise and sensitive Wisconsin poet Lorine Niedecker titled a book of poetry simply *My Friend Tree*, and it is time that I acknowledge the influence, the friendship of this American beech, sending down roots, producing buds and leaves, and hosting starlings, grackles, and other songbirds, as I, within the spell, weave with words.

In his meditative book-length essay *The Tree*, the English novelist John Fowles observes: "Achieving a relationship with nature is both a science and an art, beyond mere knowledge or mere feeling alone." I have been lucky to begin and end each day in a room embraced by an elegant beech tree, and I suppose my daily work—the practice of agriculture—can be a very good way to approach such a relationship, primarily because one is exposed to what nature is made of: sun, soil, water, wind, roots, stems, flowers, seed. But so often the sense of purpose, intrinsic to agriculture—something I have praised for many years, now having found it—can also obscure what may be purposeless in nature, at least in the sense that we use that word. Deborah Light, who donated to the Peconic Land Trust the fertile land that I have farmed for three decades, later in life became a Wiccan priestess (she embodied the role before it became official). She attended the Parliament of the World's Religions several times, sharing the stage with Nelson Mandela and the Dalai Lama in Cape Town, South Africa. Wicca is a neo-pagan, earth-revering religion, and Deborah was pleased to be known as a hedgewitch (I too love the tangles of hedges, having worked in the cliff meadows of Cornwall, bounded by hedges, of both fuchsia and stone). I learned as much from Deborah's way of being in the world as I have from the study of conservation ethics and practice. The intrinsic value of land and the diverse species that inhabit the land, both plant and animal, macro life-forms and microbial life, is based on something much greater, more expansive than "best use" or market fluctuations, and to intuit that value, to be taught by it and learn from it, requires something beyond the human effort we are presently devoting to it. If the natural world, the whole substantial pageant (to rephrase Shakespeare), exists for a purpose, that purpose is not solely ours to order or to legislate, and to achieve a relationship requires an openness to both the seen and the unseen.

It is wise for a farmer or gardener to be cognizant of the unseen, the organic matter under the surface of the soil that they hope to stimulate. Since first reading Sir Albert Howard (*The Soil and Health*) and Lady Eve Balfour (*The Living Soil*), I have been keenly aware of the macro life-forms that populate the soil beneath us: earthworms, springtails, pill bugs, millipedes, mites, beetles, and nematodes to name a few. And Sir Albert detailed the important function of mycorrhizae—fungi that enrich plant roots through a symbiotic relationship, part of what he named the "Wheel of Life." But I have been less attentive to the microbial life that inhabits this underground universe, what David R. Montgomery and Anne Biklé call the hidden half of nature. Their book by that title, addressing a new way to look at the natural world, begins with this sentence: "We are living through a scientific revolution as illuminating as the discovery that Earth orbits the Sun."

It is only very recently that our science has begun to explore an ecosystem that we have largely ignored. Not surprisingly, we have focused on the macroscopic world—forests, plains and steppes, riparian zones, wetlands, streams, and rivers—but there is a whole community beneath the soil some have likened to the dark matter that populates so much of our universe, the undefined substance that the astrophysicist Neil deGrasse Tyson refers to as "a strange, invisible friend." The recently formed Earth Microbiome Project is setting out to map the unseen world below, and to learn more of microbial partnerships that illumine the mystery of our own origin, just as physicists and cosmologists look above to the stars, and to space.

What we cannot see, the unseen that surrounds us, not only below but above and within us, predates us by over 3.6 billion years. It was then that the first organisms, known as archaea—once assumed to be bacteria—sprang into life. The five main types of microbial life—archaea, bacteria, fungi, protists, and viruses—are incredibly adaptable, and in various forms exist everywhere. It is estimated that one half the weight of life on earth is made up of microbes: ten to the thirtieth of them, or a nonillion, to use another term. They exist in each drop of water, and in every grain of sand, according to Montgomery, a geomorphologist, and Biklé, a biologist. It was Antoni van Leeuwenhoek, the owner of a drapery shop in Delft, Holland, who is credited with the discovery of microbes, circa 1676. By peering into a microscope that he had crafted himself, he found a community of animalcules that led him to investigate one substance after another. Over the course of a very long life, van Leeuwenhoek succeeded in convincing London's Royal Society that there existed a microscopic world parallel to the world our eyes register, if only we looked more closely. Fast-forward three centuries, to the late 1970s, when biophysicist Carl Woese also turned his enquiring mind to the world of microbes. Eventually Woese proposed a new way of classifying life by introducing a category above the level of kingdom known as the domain. Two of the three domains— Archaea and Bacteria—are microbial; we share the third domain, Eukarya, with all other animals, plants, and fungi. For centuries those active in the sciences have continued to gaze and theorize and classify, and so to discover or reveal the very minute organisms, our ancestors, that are synonymous with life.

The achievements of *Homo sapiens*—across all disciplines—are certainly extraordinary (as a species we are acquainted with pride), but as John Fowles observes: "Evolution has turned man into a sharply isolating creature, seeing the world not only anthropocentrically but singly, mirroring the way we like to think of our private selves." A more precise classification or understanding of the natural world—from microbe to mountain—need not necessarily diminish the understanding imagined, accumulated, written, and expressed over thousands of years in stories and mythologies, in dance, song, and theater, though it may in fact deceive us, not only about our private selves but also about our interdependency with many "strange and invisible friends."

Many times, daily, I rub shoulders with the beech tree as I pass going outward to our nearby fields, or going inward to my desk. No longer does the ground interfere with my friendship for the whole being of this graceful living thing. The British author-adventurer Robert MacFarlane reminds us that the roots of a tree can spread as wide as the tree's canopy. He writes of the underland "as a perfect inversion of the human realm, with the ground always as a mirror line." The Swiss psychologist Carl Jung, who explored archetypes, dreams, and poetic metaphor, wrote that life itself is like a plant that "lives on its rhizome." What is aboveground may last only a single season, but hidden from us, beneath the soil surface, "underneath the eternal flux," the rhizome endures.

The starlings and grackles with their frenzied autumn music have moved on to winter in a warmer place, the spiky husks of the beechnuts are scattered on the forest floor, and the papery beech leaves that hold to the tree for so long now cover the fallen leaves of oaks and hickories, a carbon carpet for passing whitetail deer. Deborah Light too has moved on, after eighty years on this earth, though she still communicates through the story of this beech tree. The particular, precise language that speaks through this tree is "beyond mere knowledge or mere feeling alone," and the syntactical structure is fostered by both what is seen and what is unseen: bark, leaves, and nuts, a network of microbial and mycelial life support beneath the soil. A few hundred years ago—with gratitude to the beech—I may have used some thin bark to serve as a tablet. I imagine I would have carved the same words I now type, words I have learned in the surrounding fields, as I have plowed and cultivated the same soil that animates this tree, or set seeds into it. I write: "This landscape is crisp within earth's spin." Words that begin a book. And like the noise of starlings, like earthworms, archaea, the effervescence of spring leaves, the sweet meat of beechnuts, all a part of an earthen gift, in the words of the author John Hay, "one of the earth's inexhaustible ways of seeing."

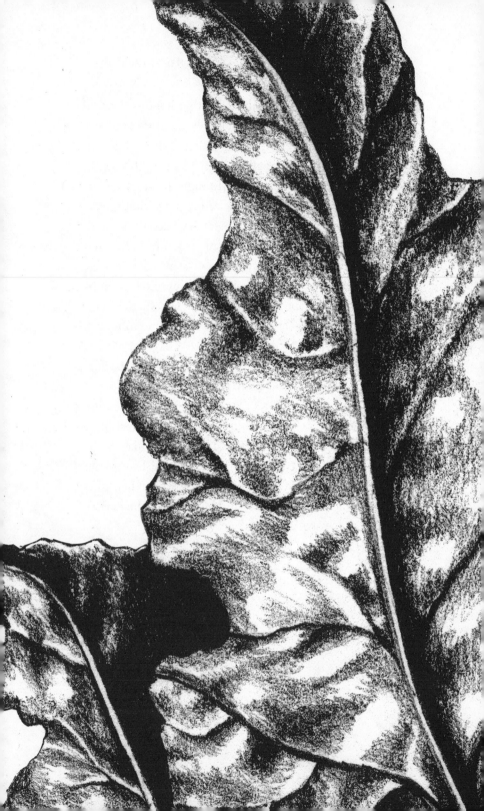

Chapter 2

TONGUES IN TREES, BOOKS
IN THE RUNNING BROOKS

Divine and formless is the Spirit,
which is outside and inside, unborn, not breath, not mind,
pure, higher than the high imperishable . . .
from it flow rivers of all kinds . . .

—*MUNDAKA UPANISHAD*

And, O moon,
As we travail to sleep we do not know whether, with your
genius furthering us,
We should be counted as the cuspid waves of the seas, or as
the souls of trees
Whose leaves we are, growing for you, the crowded
summits stark, heavenly.

—LOUIS ZUKOFSKY, "25," *29 POEMS*

In a story told by the Lakota medicine man Leonard Crow Dog, when the Great Unknown Power, identi-fied by the name Unknowingly, had finished planting the seed of life—after a half million eons of creation time—he then planted trees (the evergreens, pine and cedar). The trees spoke to one another, in an unknown language: "Every day and every moment they were talking." After another three million years of creation time, the Great Sun sensed that the time was ripe for caretakers to enter the world, for humans to meet their green relations.

On my daily walk down to the Saco River in a certain woodland in Maine, I overheard this unknown language, a conversation among ash and maple, oak, birch, poplar, and spruce, stirred by the wind and the sound of a river. It was a subtle language, and since I had been raised in the suburbs of western New York, the timbre and music of the woods were new and the words to name them unfamiliar. I was unaware that an underground social network exists in a forest, but I felt it, and now, decades later, forest ecologists such as Suzanne Simard, a self-proclaimed "forest detective," have conducted research and experiments to learn how and why trees "talk" to one another. Over the course of a summer, and for several years after, I listened to the local signals of the wood wide web on my way down to the waters of the Saco, on a path that led through a mixed forest undisturbed for a few generations. The siren song: cool water, the cleansing current of the Saco, a stillness felt in this northern woodland.

I had followed friends to Buxton, near the hamlet of Bar Mills, and to a plot of land near the end of a gravel road, to learn the very basics of homesteading (a handsome word) and restoration. We met and worked together at a rambling inn on the coast, a skip along the rocks from the Bush family compound. I arrived in Maine by a circuitous route; a few years after college, restless, and at the suggestion of my poet mentor, I had packed my books and my Brittany spaniel companion, Purdah, into my vintage (a kind word for it) VW and set off in search of a graduate degree, at a school in North Carolina. Upon arrival, all appeared alien: the town, the campus, even the thought of reentering a classroom. This was not the place to begin again. I opened my tattered map—a colorful road map, accordion style, with personality—closed my eyes, and circled with my index finger; it came to rest on an unfamiliar place, though the name had a familial, playful, contrapuntal quality: Kennebunkport. Reverse direction, return to the North, so soon? I chose to follow the map.

We worked long hours at the inn, and the tips were generous. W. and S., a married couple raised in rural Wisconsin, were a few years older, and with their savings they were anxious to find land and a house, a home they could call their own. At that time, at least in southern Maine, $6,000 and a pioneer spirit were the price for three acres and a house still standing after a century and a half. A homestead is a house with outbuildings, and this one was a classic example, circa the early 1800s. Early on, W., aware of a tradition outside my realm of knowledge, guessed that we would find a coin, somewhere within the walls, a talisman placed to honor the structure and those who raised it. Nestled behind a thick rambling lilac hedge and an ancient leaning apple tree, the farmhouse was a New England Cape in need of tender care. It was a double initiation for a young traveler—following four years of liberal arts—into the practical use of hammer and axe, and to the demands of January and February in the Maine woods.

To recognize and to name trees, to identify varied species, was a daily study, and also a necessity in preparation for the long winter: we heated (with a Norwegian Jøtul) and cooked and baked (on a cast-iron Glenwood) with wood. Although my sympathies, then and now, align with the expression of Thoreau, that trees "are good for other things than boards and shingles," the old farmhouse needed both. I may have scanned Thoreau's journals and *The Maine Woods* at the time, though now his words have a seasoned resonance: "something like the woodland sounds will be heard to echo through the leaves of a good book." Camping out on the second floor—which I reached by a ladder—I devoted my evenings to readings tracing my Irish lineage: W. B. Yeats ("Who will go drive with Fergus now, / And pierce the deep wood's woven shade"), and the experimental, melodious prose of James Joyce. I was captivated at the time by the banter of two washerwomen on the banks of the river Liffey, a scene expressive of the sound of rivers ("Tell me, tell me, tell me, elm! Night night! Telmetale of stem or stone. Beside the rivering waters of, hitherandthithering waters of Night!"), but as I remember now, by day it was not a literary language I was attentive to, but the hitherandthithering waters of the river I reached through the woods, the Saco.

The name Saco is a derivation of an Abenaki word meaning "flowing out" or "outlet." Although there is discussion concerning the identity of the Indigenous people who lived along the lower Saco and near the mouth of the river, several sources identify these people as the Sokoki (known in their own language as the Ozogwakiak, "breakaway people"). The Abenaki are one of five principal nations of the Wabanaki Confederacy, a linguistic and geographic grouping with a shared language: Algonquian. The French cartographer Samuel de Champlain referred to them as Almouchiquois. The Sokoki, a nomadic tribe that traveled seasonally between the mouth of the river and Mount Washington, were members of the Tortoise Clan of the eastern Algonquians. In a land of abundance bordering the ocean, they were hunter-gatherers, farmers, and fishers, and they had lived along the coast—of what is now Maine—for twelve thousand years before Europeans arrived. Wabanaki villages were always located along rivers, and an individual's way of being in the world, of identifying with land and with self, was based on one's home watershed. The Wabanaki homeland is a broad expanse of the Northeast coastal region, extending into present-day Canada, including the Mi'kmaq, Maliseet, Passamaquoddy, and the Penobscot people. Abenaki: "whitening sky at daybreak, dawnland."

The Italian explorer Giovanni da Verrazano, who came into contact with the Abenaki in 1524, expressed wonder when he first encountered this land of "mightie greate wooddes . . . with divers sorts of trees [as] plesaunte and delectable to beholde as is possible to imagine." Several decades later, in 1605, Samuel de Champlain, known as the father of New France, who explored the North Atlantic coast up and down, drew an expressive map of the mouth of the Saco, showing cornfields on either side of the river, along with Abenaki wigwams and longhouses. He seems to have taken artistic pleasure in his mapmaking: adjacent to numbers that report the harbor sounding depths, he included a sea creature, dragon-like, an emblem of wildness, for this was an undiscovered country to the Europeans. Not so for the Abenaki, who had been on speaking terms with this wildness for thousands of years. *Cartographer*, from the Greek: "leaf of paper" + "writer," one who makes or compiles charts or maps. To make a map—even one as artful as Champlain's—initiates not only exploration but exploitation of a kind new to an old continent strangely renamed as the New World.

The Saco rises at two thousand feet above sea level at Crawford Notch, a major pass through the White Mountains of the Granite State, New Hampshire. The intrusions that formed this range, inclusive of the tallest peak in the East, Mount Washington (Agiocochook, "home of the great spirit"), were created over a hundred million years ago. Evidence of glacial movement is visible as shapely cirques and striations in the metamorphic and igneous rock. Because so many rivers have their sources in the White Mountains—the Connecticut, Pemigewasset, Merrimack, Androscoggin, and the Saco, among others—New Hampshire has an alternate name, one I favor: the Mother of Rivers. As this one water child, Sakohki, emerges from Saco Lake, it flows within the granite and drops rapidly—600 feet in the first 3 miles; then the river descends through a series of falls to eventually empty into the Atlantic, at Saco Bay, 136 miles southeast from the Notch. Along the way, the Saco drains an area of 1,700 square miles of field and forest.

Aldo Leopold, ecologist and writer, penned an essay in 1924 called "The River of the Mother of God," a title that has been on my mind so long I have forgotten when I first heard it (an echo of Leopold's words). His essay is a lament for our species' failure to protect the last vestiges of earth's wilderness. But Leopold opens his piece with gratitude for the gifts of a neighboring continent and "the trackless Amazonian forest." Gratitude for rare woods, pleasant fruits, for coffee, for "the dawn-wind rustling in autumnal trees." Above all, he is grateful for the story of a mighty river that flows into a forest, and disappears. In this story the Spanish captain who named the river Río Madre de Dios, journeys inland, like the river, and he too disappears. The graphic of this tale shows on a map as a heavy dotted line that meanders through mountains, a river with no beginning and no end. And it is that river—at once a symbol of unknown places and of our human drive for conquest—that suggests to Leopold our human history "is but a succession of adventures into the Unknown." Though I can name the source and the mouth and the flow of the Saco before our conquest of it, the rain, the mountain runoff, and the falls and eddies through mineral rock impart a name and a spirit that stream within it still. The effervescence of that water bathed my body daily as I swam the wide river from east to west and back, most often alone, near dusk.

Champlain crossed and recrossed the Atlantic more than twenty times early in the seventeenth century. After voyaging as far south as Cape Cod, he redirected his energy and exploration on waterways and land to the north, and upon sailing up the Saint Lawrence river, he colonized the land that became Quebec in 1608 (*kebec*: "the narrowing of the waters"). English explorers were not far behind the French—in 1614, Captain John Smith arrived at the mouth of the Saco, and he was followed not long after by one of the earliest English settlements in what became known as New England. For fifty years or so, the early colonists and the Indigenous people shared in what non-Indigenous historians have called a peaceful coexistence, though the arrival of the English had upset the balance of trade between the French and the Native tribes. As settlements grew in size, the Abenaki, exposed to virulent diseases and increasing numbers of colonists, were forced to move farther north and east, farther from the land where the river comes out.

The U.S. logging industry was born in the forests of Maine and New Hampshire—the first sawmill along the Saco River was built in 1650. Within 150 years that number had grown to 17, and the Saco swelled with wood, floating, drifting and stalling, churning to mill or market. The wood of choice for the early colonists—and for those who viewed the dense Northern forests as so many board feet—was the white pine. In time Maine came to be known as the Pine Tree State. *Pinus strobus*, one of more than 90 species of pine trees, is admired for its elegant height, and for its adaptability. In his book *American Canopy*, subtitled *Trees, Forests, and the Making of a Nation*, Eric Rutkow highlights a quality of this conifer that led to the overharvest of the once-dense Northern woodlands: "And unlike logs cut from hardwoods, those from white pines floated easily upon water, an invaluable quality in a young nation where rivers functioned as commercial highways." The white pine is the tallest tree in the Northeast, and as such, after the arrival of Captain Smith and Captain George Weymouth (who carried seeds from Maine back to England) early in the seventeenth century, it was prized for the durable ship masts much needed by the British Royal Navy. The explorer James Rosier, in 1605, wrote in his journal: "Upon the hills grow notable high timber trees, masts for ships of 400 tun." The British Navy designed and built new cargo ships for the purpose of transporting massive pines across the Atlantic. Britain was the first nation in the modern era to exhaust their supply of wood; already, early in the seventeenth century, the country experienced a national shortage of timber. John Evelyn, author of *Sylva* (a bestselling book in the seventeenth century), addressed the shortage as a national crisis in 1664: "We had better be without gold than without timber." He urged that trees must be planted to restore the health of the land. Adopting his phrase three centuries later, Henry Hobhouse notes that trees have the unique ability to "reclothe the land." Evelyn would agree with the assessment of our contemporary author Fred Hageneder, included in his *The Spirit of Trees*:

> All human civilization and culture has been built—and still is—on the use of fire and wood. Trees provided their very bodies to cushion humanity's development. Everywhere it went, humankind could only survive because trees had come before them. This direct reliance on trees has been the longest dependency in the cultural history of humankind.

Henry Hobhouse, in *Seeds of Wealth*, attributes the arrival of the industrial revolution in Britain—fifty to one hundred years ahead of any other country—to an insufficient supply of homegrown wood (they turned to the manufacture of charcoal).

Rather than the calculating eye of the royal shipbuilders, I prefer the appreciation of *Pinus strobus* expressed by Thoreau: "There is no finer tree." Jane Johnston

Schoolcraft (Bamewawage Zhikaquay), the daughter of
an Ojibwe mother and a Scottish Irish father and considered to be among the first known Native women writers,
agreed with Thoreau. Returning from Europe, and upon
sighting land and this magnificent conifer, she was ec-
static: "Zhingwaak, zhingwaak, nos sa!" (The pine, the
pine, my father!)

The Haudenosaunee, whose land lies to the west of
Lake Champlain and near the shores of Lake Ontario
and Lake Erie, named it "the tree of peace"—the five
green needles, held in a bundle along each branch,
symbolized the original five Nations of the Iroquois
Confederacy. Robin Wall Kimmerer observes that
the white pine in the Anishinabe language is spoken
of as a respected person, zhingwaak, with multiple
roles in Native stories—as a virtuous being and as a
protector of humans. The tallest, strongest pines were
honored by Indigenous people as Elders. In the center
of a beaded belt—the Hiawatha Wampum—stands
the white pine as an image of law and peace. When
Deganawidah banished the Evil Mind, the bringer of
discord and war, he taught a new philosophy of the
Good Mind. Deganawidah planted a pine and spoke of
the four great white roots that would grow out in four
directions, spreading the precepts of the Good Mind—
Righteousness (Gaiwoh), Health (Skenon), and Power
(Gashasdenshaa). Our democracy—fragile as it is at
this moment—whose founding structure is based on
the governance of the Haudenosaunee Confederacy,
may still draw strength from the white pine, but the tree
needs protection; it must be watered and nourished.

By the 1830s, New York had replaced Maine as the nation's largest supplier of timber, and as the next wave of settlers moved westward, the more aggressive logging interests also shifted away from the Northeast to the Great Lakes states, and eventually to the West Coast. Still, throughout the next century the banks and midriver of the Saco were lined with gristmills, sawmills, tanneries, and eventually dams, to provide hydroelectric power. At one time forty-four dams slowed or served to harness the generous water flow that descends from Crawford Notch. Within two hundred years of the first European settlements, the landscape and ecology of the Northeast coast had been radically altered, and in a book published in 1864, George Perkins Marsh, named the father of the modern conservation movement, had something to say about this brand of colonial "progress." A Vermont diplomat, linguist, and naturalist, Marsh wrote: "Man has too long forgotten that the earth was given to him for usufruct alone, not for consumption, still less for profligate waste." *Usufruct*, a word of Latin origin, sounds strange today (and perhaps also for readers in 1864), but Marsh's choice was accurate, the exact word he wanted: "the right of enjoying the use and advantages of another's property short of destruction or waste of its substance" (from the *Oxford English Dictionary*). Whose property it was, and is today, is a question we all should consider, and there is an expanding conversation in progress today among the Native peoples of Maine and those of diverse lineage who arrived later. (First Light is a collaboration between conservationists and Penobscot, Passamaquoddy, Maliseet, and Mi'kmaq communities who seek to expand Wabanaki access to and stewardship of land. Collaboration and reciprocity is at the center of their work: "relearning, recentering, and returning at the speed of trust.")

Clear-cutting and overcutting continue to the present day, though Maine is now the most forested state in the country. Notably, remarkably, 90 percent of the state's land is now covered with trees, but the figures reflect three centuries of settlement, clearing, and industry, not restraint: only 3 percent of Maine's forest is late successional and only 0.1 percent is old growth. And now we know—though the evidence has been offered for decades—that the preservation and restoration of forests is one of the primary tools we possess to address climate disruption.

When we quote statistics, as a useful measure of where we are, we commonly neglect the movement of time beyond the reach of our (mortal) comprehension. In an essay titled "They Carry Us with Them: The Great Tree Migration," Chelsea Steinauer-Scudder observes: "But trees—or, more appropriately, forests—are perhaps not so rooted, so reliably *placed*, as we might think. Right now, around the world, trees are on the move." She traces the northward journey of spruce trees beginning at the end of the Pleistocene, 14,600 years ago, as the weather warmed and glaciers receded. By the time of the Holocene, 3,000 years later, spruce stepped into Maine and farther into Canada, as pines, also traveling up from the south, replaced the spruce in Maine. Fast-forward another 6,000 years (though pause to consider the actual pace of ecosystem variation), and, after an extended period of drought, as hemlock disappears, spruce pedals southward to occupy the boundaries we are familiar with. In the evolution of species, such movement is not new, but

we have ramped up the rate of change. Due to climate disruption, the atmospheric CO_2 concentration of 419 parts
per million has reached the highest level our planet has
known for 3 to 5 million years. In the Northeast alone,
86 species of trees are on the move, both north and west.
Can we learn sufficient respect for these species to preserve forests that are in motion?

"Poetry, like music, is to be heard. It deals in sound—
long sounds and short sounds, heavy beats and light
beats, the tone relation of vowels." Inspired by the
teaching of the Northumbrian poet Basil Bunting, and
by the music in his odes, I was at work on the craft, flush
with the sounds of this woodland place, the path to the
river, and I wrote:

> He slows at the oak tier—
> Yards to the river. Near, a beech
> Waves, leaf left of winter's chafe.

The tree species I came to know best over my first
winter in Maine, white ash, was intermixed, prominent
among the oaks, birch, maple, and spruces. Occupied
with removing walls, building walls, replacing windows,
insulating, we had no time to gather a store of firewood.
As the first snows began to fall, we learned to wade
through drifts to collect wood, to stack a week's supply

under the overhang of the shed. Softwood will not burn long, especially when green (newly cut or felled), and most of the northern hardwoods must be seasoned—excepting ash. *Fraxinus americana* is a lovely white wood, it grows straight and tall, it has a low moisture content, and it splits easily. Wonderfully springy it has been called—my bat of choice, I remember, and I still hear the resonant sound as hardball meets hardwood. In Maine, and during the winter especially, another common use is more to the point— ash is often fashioned into axe handles. I learned to split ash wood as fuel for the Jøtul and heat for the home, with an ash axe handle in hand.

Unknown to me at the time, by this gesture I was near to the wisdom of two poets, one my near contemporary and a fellow citizen of Turtle Island, and another who dwelled in China, seventeen hundred years ago. Gary Snyder titled his 1983 book of poems *Axe Handles*, and the beginning poem quotes a phrase Snyder learned from Ezra Pound, who learned it from Lu Chi, author of *Wen Fu* (*The Art of Writing*):

"In making the handle
  Of an axe
  By cutting wood with an axe
  The model is indeed near at hand."

Lu Chi's third-century text (to surface again in a future chapter) is a primer on the art of writing. With a Northern woodland as my teacher and an open notebook on my oak desk in the newly gutted Maine Cape, centuries of craft and introspection aligned, taking shape as an ode:

Sand bed pockets stone, constant

Of flood led into thicket.
Silken marks the young leaf.
Dry weeds crest in her hair
though he sees wet roots on her bed.

The sound of moving water and wind through the trees gave birth to Sanskrit poetry. The word for writing in Sanskrit derives from the word for the ash tree. The botanical name for ash, *Fraxinus*, likely derives from the Latin *frango* ("I break"), an action Shakespeare had in mind when he composed (in *Coriolanus*) this musical line: "My grained ash an hundred times hath broke / And scarr'd the moon with splinters." The single-bladed seed of the ash, known as a samara (a word I love) was called *avis lingua* ("bird's tongue") by the Romans. For centuries, ash wood has been used for walking sticks, canoe paddles, lances and spears, bows, arrows, and, by Northern Native people, for snowshoes and baskets. In a legend of the Wabanaki the ash starred the earth with people. Their creator, Glooscap, a great warrior, carved arrow shafts from ash heartwood. When he pierced a champion white ash with a tempered arrow, the first humans poured out of the tree to inhabit our planet. Enrique Salmón, in *Iwígara: The Kinship of Plants and People*, notes that tools made of ash are sometimes thought "to have a spirit, or to be alive," as was the ash wood I came to know. And for me it did indeed sing—in the grove, and, after it was felled, in the woodstove. We returned the ash to the garden, in anticipation of spring.

The Norse tree of life, Yggdrasil, is often character-
ized as an ash tree. Yet the Norse *Edda* (circa 1200 CE)
describe the world tree as the evergreen-needle ash—not
at all an accurate naming of the species *Fraxinus*, a deciduous broadleaf wherever it chooses to root. It is more
likely that the sky god Odin suspended himself upside
down not from an ash, but from the limb of a yew tree—
the yew is an evergreen, with needles, and known also
as the tree of life (one among many species so named,
an encouraging sign in my mind). After nine days and
nights, Odin, bound to a tree unknown to any man, spies
the Runes, a magical alphabet of letters and concepts. In
circular, mythological fashion the ash (or yew) tree shares
with Odin in the transformative magic as he gathers the
Runes and falls,

> Well-being I won
> And wisdom too.
> I grew and took joy in my growth:
> From a word to a word
> I was led to a word,
> From a deed to another deed.

I return in vivid memory to the path that led through
an undulating meadow, past the sheds, past the chicken
pen, the rabbit hutch, the shelter for Nancy the sow with
her latest litter, then to the edge of the wood thicket

before the river, and to the tone relation of sounds within the woods, stirred by wind and moisture rising from the river:

> He picks the pulp of apple root—
> sweats in sun, brushes shad, broods
> in the wood among ore and shade—
> Sun, for her bed, turn the root pulp red.

As a novice in the Maine forest, and with the forms that words make, I had begun to listen: something drew me there. The clearest sound came from the water that sluiced through granite at Crawford Notch, an echo alive in the river's current. And from the hyphal network, underground, I sensed another kind of expression. An ancient language quieted by the noise of four centuries of exploration, conquest, settlement, overharvest, commerce . . . but still there, weaving through soil and the seasonal fall of leaves and needles feeding the underground. What I came to recognize in these woods prepared me for a future avocation I did not anticipate, that of a community farmer and conservationist. The underground fungal web that connects the forest as a community provides invaluable lessons for building human community. My time in the Maine woods served as a touchstone for my life's work: to nurture fertile soils, to cultivate plants, to nourish a reciprocal relationship with all species.

In my room, in the 1811 farmhouse (we found the coin), by dim light, I read and searched for the cadences at the heart of an art: The art of poetry is "the accurate transmission of feeling through words." Perhaps that is what the trees are always doing, though *feeling* and *words* are our words to describe what cannot be articulated. So what do ash, oak, maple, birch, hickory, and a river have to teach? Listen to the chatter of two washerwomen at the ford (imagined by an Irish author remembering, in Trieste, the lisps of the Liffey): "Well, you know or don't you kennet or haven't I told you every telling has a taling and that's the he and the she of it. Look, look, the dusk is growing! My branches lofty are taking root." The river carries the cadence of its source and its return to the sea within its flow and falls, it carries the glide of birch-bark canoes and the slow flow of great pine logs, the labor of those who built the dams, of fishers and trappers, and the trees, through reaching branches and roots in riverine earth, possess the collective memory. A proverb of the Maori people of the Te Urewera rain forest in New Zealand praises the connection between a human and flowing water: "I am the river and the river is me."

This is the art I still wake to, daily: to make, by breath, sweet music. I heard it there, in the land of the People of the Dawn. And writing here now, surrounded by oaks and pines, I am drawn back by a photograph: Daisy at the river! After so many moves and years, the shadowy figure of a blissful farm dog enters the sunlit opening to the river, and I return there. And yes, imagining the lives of those who found dwelling along the river that flows from Crawford Notch to the sea, I am aware of the words of Heraclitus, "It is impossible to step twice into the same river." James Joyce plucked a composite word out of the air (after decades of linguistic study), *mememormee*, and it leads me, changed, back to the Saco, and to the path that leads through the woods. The trees are reaching for light, searching for nutrients, like us, and the path is thick with last year's growth, the things that have fallen to feed the following spring. Another language to learn—it abides in the canopy and in the mycelium network, always available to us; though, in search of short-term profit, or in avoidance of relationships, we often exclude this natural music.

I chose to follow a road map, and eventually the way led through an open meadow, along a path thick with needles of conifers and leaves of maple and ash, through a restored wood along the banks of a river passing through time and flowing out. Many before me had traveled that path, and some, as caretakers, listened for the wind in the branches and a voice that dwells among the roots. Someone among the Abenaki heard that the trees "every day and every moment were talking" and she or he imagined a way to harmonize:

> We are the stars who sing, we sing with our light;
> We are the birds of fire, we fly over the sky.
> Our light is a voice.
> We make a road for the spirits,
> for the spirits to pass over.

Chapter 3

A CARE FOR WORDS

What motion of the sun or stream
Or eyelid shot the gleam
That pierced my body through?

—W. B. YEATS, "STREAM AND SUN AT GLENDALOUGH"

Let's begin with heather, which corresponds to the eighteenth letter of the ancient Celtic Ogham alphabet, Ur, meaning "all that is fresh, green, renewing, liberal, generous, free." Let's attempt to repeat the name in Gaelic, *Fraoch more*, and in colloquial English, ling: "Still keeps the Ling its darksome green / Thick set with little flowers." A member of the heath family, Ericaceae, heather is the sole species of the genus *Calluna* (from the Greek *kalluno*: "to cleanse or adorn"). From a distance—say a perch on an upper limb of a rare oak—the rolling hills of Wicklow, bearing thousands of tiny bellflowers, swell as a purple sea. For the Druids, as for present lovers of the heath, this is a sacred landscape.

According to botanist Diana Beresford-Kroeger, heather is the botanical body of the heath. Under the purple heather lies a mix of acid soil, of sand and peat: an ancient ice sheet scoured rock to make sand, while peat is the humus gift of trees. Educated in the Brehon

Law in the Lisheens Valley in County Cork, Beresford-Kroeger writes: "Heathland is one last memory held in the soil of the ancient forest system of the planet." There is an ethereal quality to the landscape produced, should we need to define it, by arbutin, an aerosol that rises from soil and plant. Out of that soil memory and vapor, songs are made.

Seamus Heaney, the Irish master poet, acknowledged his study in *scoileanna scairte*, the hedge school of Wicklow where he composed his "Glanmore Sonnets." In a later poem, "Postscript," Heaney suggests a pilgrimage: "And some time make the time to drive out west / Into County Clare, along the Flaggy Shore." I made the time, or I was led by time, to pedal through County Wicklow and the purple heath toward the west, propelled by two wheels rather than four, and I met Heaney along the way.

I bought the bike in Blessington after a summer in a writing course held at the Divinity Hostel, Rathgar, on the outskirts of Dublin. The honorary title "the oldest bicycle in Ireland" has been claimed at least once—Ballymoss she was called, named after a champion racehorse; Jim McGrath bought her for thirty bob and pedaled her for sixty years, an estimated fifty thousand miles. Had I been aware of this ranking, mine may have been in the running. Her name was Maura.

Blessington was the nearest village to the hilly sanctuary of Suzanna and Bill's farm (aunt and uncle of our program director); after a week of seminars and study, I was among the students of the Antioch Summer Program that found freedom there in haymaking. Suzanna and her family benefited from the labor, and she fed us, mothered us, shared blessings with us. As a child raised in the post-WWII suburbs of Tonawanda, New York, by a mother born in Ireland, I felt the landscape of Wicklow come in close, like an embrace.

I set off for the west after an extremely rare summer of sun for the Emerald Isle—six weeks of it, to be exact, a surprise to Irish citizens to be sure, and to peat and plants. Inside my canvas satchel, strapped above the back wheel, I carried a change of clothes, a notebook, a few books, and a sleeping bag. My destination on the first day, after a long climb into the Wicklow hills, was a youth hostel on the route toward Cashel.

The long string of sunny days came to an end the very day my ride began, and the change was dramatic, not uncommon in the North Atlantic, as if the clouds had been building a reserve. On the exposed high ground of Wicklow, I met the precise word *lashing* in the form of rain and wind—in an instant I was wet, skin and bones and satchel. A covey of Calibans designed the next event—a nail. On a narrow country road, perfectly placed to slow a hopeful traveler? My tire picked it up; I dismounted and walked for miles, through sheets of rain, to reach the hostel.

The matron at the door took one look at me, and with no pity in her bearing asked, "Did you reserve a place?"

"No."

"In that case we can't accommodate you," she said, guarding the door.

"Oh," I replied, dripping.

Silence, a most worshipful thing, admired by poets as a word, as a form in the air, or as an element preliminary to words, acted in my favor.

After what seemed like several minutes, face-to-face, she opened the door and with no visible emotion offered: "We'll find a place for you."

I awoke in the morning to sun, and to kindness served as a bowl of steaming oatmeal. I repaired the tire and set off through the gentle hills toward Glendalough. Midmorning I stopped to rest in a handsome dip of the road, a valley enveloped by heather, and walked out into the sea of ling, to immerse in the heath. Even to an untrained eye, the small circle of white bellflowers among the purple appeared as a gift. I plucked a few stems, tied the white bouquet to the handlebars of my vintage black bike, and, renewed, pedaled on. I remembered Yeats: "What made me live like these that seem / self-born, born anew?"

Only later did I learn how rare it is to find the stems of white bellflowers among the dominant purple ("as rare as hen's teeth," according to Beresford-Kroeger). When white heather is offered as a gift, the one who receives it inherits luck, and as the saying goes, that gift will carry on throughout a life. My concern that day was the immediate road ahead—if unaware of the blessing of white heather, I was fully awake to the place, the touch and smell of Wicklow peat and the botanical body of the heath.

I pedaled on toward the Rock of Cashel, a cluster of medieval buildings on a limestone outcrop in Tipperary South, my chosen route. At a crossroads, one sign pointed toward Cashel, the other toward an unfamiliar town, Kilkenny. Strangely, inexplicably, I took the turn toward the latter town, my hands guided by the handlebars or the heather. The town was filled with a festive energy; Kilkenny Arts Week (I was unaware) was in progress. Seamus Heaney was the Arts Week poet in residence, and that evening in Kilkenny Castle he would introduce Eugène Guillevic, a French poet known as the poet of Carnac.

Here I pause my journey to Kerry to return to an office on the campus of Cornell University, Ithaca, New York, six months or so previously. In a meeting with a young professor, the poet Robert Morgan, as we discussed words and he read aloud some of my lines, he stopped to ask: "Have you read Seamus Heaney?"

I looked for Heaney's poetry, not readily available at the time. Once I found his printed work, I opened first to this, from an elegy for a composer friend:

> The gunwale's lifting ear—
> trusting the gift,
> risking gift's undertow—
> is unmanned now
>
> but one whole afternoon
> it was deep in both our weights.

and the connection was made. In the first poem of my own *Book of Odes*, I had recently penned the same phrase, "deep in both our weights." I met with Morgan again, flush with excitement. His immediate response: "You should write to him!"

With some hesitancy, I wrote a letter, found an address in Ireland, and sent it off. Then, by chance—in the interim airpost time—I enrolled in the course that opened for a summer in Dublin; in September the course would be centered in London. My letter traveled to Ireland, though Heaney was by then teaching for a semester in California. He received my letter in Berkeley and kindly replied to my return address—Watertown, Massachusetts. But I was in Dublin, and poetic justice was in our favor: his letter found me at the Divinity Hostel.

"Nice to find the language *deep in both our weights*," he wrote. "Thank you for writing and sending the poem, which has a cleanliness and care for words that I go for." Sweet words to the ears of a young poet! (Decades later, the red felt-tip script is still quite legible, including his PS: "This is the only pen I have just now—sorry.")

I plucked the white bough of heather and was led to the ancient town on the river Nore. That evening, in the castle, Heaney, a child of Derry, presented his friend Guillevic, a poet of French "peasant stock" who later received the Prix Goncourt. Guillevic was born in the village of Carnac on the Morbihan peninsula of southern Brittany (Bretagne), a province named Armorica by the Romans, a place of stark beauty settled by Celtic peoples.

Like Cornwall, and like much of Ireland, Carnac is a place of stone. It is a land of menhirs (*men* = "stone," *hir* = "long"), dolmens, and the most concentrated site of Neolithic monuments in France (as the Cornish Penwith Peninsula is to Britain). The sea, the Atlantic channel between Cornwall and Brittany, served more as a link than a barrier between the Celtic people, and they spoke a similar dialect of Gaelic. The Carnac Alignments, estimated to be seven thousand years old, are the largest gathering of standing stones in the world, nearly three thousand granite blocks spanning almost four miles, exuding mystery. As the ancient "Song of Amergin" goes: "Who but I can unfold the secrets of the unhewn dolmen?" Who were the builders, how did they move such weight, what language did stone speak to man, what words did the builders voice as answer?

Guillevic, who read with a sweet, lulling tone, used words as a bridge between humans and nature—as if syllables and stone evolved through centuries of communion. From his poem "Where?" (in the translation by Denise Levertov):

> That which is not in stone,
> Not in the wall of stone and earth,
> Not even in trees,
> That which forever trembles a little,
>
> Must, then, be in us.

Guillevic referred to himself as *un homme de la pre-histoire* (a man from prehistory): "I am here. I exist." He was built like a menhir according to a fellow poet. His poems are austere, meditative, cleansed by wind and wave, a reflection of the landscape of Carnac, and from the land he learned the art of poetic condensation (in my preferred recipe for the art, American poet Louis Zukofsky says, "the rest is proper breathing space, ease, grace"). He read in French that evening in Kilkenny and voiced the universal language of stone, sea, and earth, and later I shared the surprise of the moment with Seamus Heaney. I cannot unfold the secrets of my ride to the west of Ireland, nor do I need to; it was a poetic pilgrimage. Echoes of the journey both preceded and still follow my actual passage. In the words of Basil Bunting: "Poetry and music are both patterns of sound drawn on a background of time." And time is a surrounding and seamless cloak, not a progression of ticks on the face of a clock.

But the reader needs more than an evocation, something more exact to gauge the author's authenticity, to weigh what is real and what desired, to embrace some clarity. The next evening in St. Canice's Cathedral, a stone space with the feel of a spacious forest grove, dating from 1251, the New Irish Chamber Orchestra performed (soaring as swallows do) a concert of Tchaikovsky's *Serenade for Strings* and Vivaldi's *Four Seasons*. In that interior space—of exquisite acoustics, where twelve hundred people can gather and listen—the music was more than an echo of the external landscape but instead an expansion of it. The cycle of days, drawn by bow and strings, moved as wind through the trees, with the ease and grace

and fury of each season, the darksome green renewing.
"The moment is dear to us," Stanley Kunitz writes, "precisely because it is so fugitive . . . Art is that chalice into
which we pour the wine of transcendence."

Years later, Heaney honored Guillevic with a poem
he titled "A Herbal":

> Between heather and marigold,
> Between sphagnum and buttercup,
> Between dandelion and broom,
> Between forget-me-not and honeysuckle,
>
> As between clear blue and cloud,
> Between haystack and sunset sky,
> Between oak tree and slated roof,
>
> I had my existence. I was there.
> Me in place and the place in me.

I made it to the west, not to County Clare, but to the
Dingle Peninsula, to a broad headland that receives the
Atlantic. I rode with purpose and abandon on the last
stretch from Tralee to the town of Dingle, pausing only to
taste blackberries, a gift of the hedges, pedaling against
"the big soft buffetings" that Heaney felt too, above the
sea in Clare. In the pub a fellow turned to me: "Two and a
half hours by cycle from Tralee . . . Bejesus!" I had earned
my glass of Guinness.

Why did I ride to Dingle, I ask myself now, what was
the urgency? The answer has everything to do with the
word that begins Guillevic's long poem titled "Carnac":

"Mer. Mer au bord du neant / Qui se mele au neant" (Sea on the edge of nothing / Who meets with nothing). An answer as ephemeral as the final slips of ocean mist that fondle the headland.

In the morning, I rode out to the place that inspired my journey—to Clogher Head, the farthest western point of mainland Ireland (*clogh*: "stone," but follow the word back to "bell" or "clock.") The sea surges on rock, and like the hands of time, the tide chimes on stone wave after wave. I heard the cadence of the heath here too, high on the headland, in the western wind that moves the waves, somewhere before words, without weight. True, Seamus, it caught my heart off guard, this "earthed lightning," a renewal that now trembles in my hands like the white bells of the letter Ur.

Chapter 4

IN THE SEASON OF GRAIN RAIN

The shuttle has worked in my heart
as it worked the hearts
of those who came before me;

continuing the same
warp and woof,
I must make my fabric new.

—LU CHI, *THE ART OF WRITING*

The plough slowly rakes soil . . .
In the essence of thick green
the cuckoo sings.

—TRADITIONAL CHINESE SONG

One of the oldest words in the Chinese language, *wen*, is linked to writing or literature as an expression of *hsin* (mind): form and meaning become one. In ancient Chinese thought, no distinction exists between heart and mind; in Taoism and Ch'an Buddhism, *hsin* connotes consciousness emptied of content, or "consciousness as empty awareness" as outlined by scholar and translator David Hinton. "And at this fundamental level," he says, "mind is nothing other than nonbeing, the pregnant

void from which all things are engendered." In the tradition of rivers-and-mountains poetry, another word,
li—which originally named the striations in a piece of
jadestone—evokes the concept of an inner pattern, an
enduring pulse of nature, a natural law that inspires a
writer to open to the currents and backwaters within
the flow of life. Lu Chi wrote:

> When the vein of jade
> is revealed in the rock,
> the whole mountain glistens.

One of the poets in this tradition, Su Tung-p'o
(Su Shih, 1037–1101) took his literary name—*Tung-p'o*
translates as "East Slope"—from the place he lived
for years as a subsistence farmer, Sichuan Province
in south-central China. Raised in a family of officials
and scholars, and influential in state government as
a young man, he later lived in solitude in the prov-
inces; he is respected as one of the finest poets in the
rivers-and-mountains tradition. East Slope observes
clouds, peaks and summits, mist, and

> cascades tumbling a hundred Ways in headlong flight,
> stitching forests and treading rock, seen and unseen
> as they plunge toward valley headwaters.

In "Crossing the Mountains," Su writes:

> Water rinses my feet, an empty mountain stream
>   murmuring,

and mist drifts into my robes, all droplets of
    kingfisher-green.

Who can let go of a mountain pheasant breaking into
    flight
across cliffwalls, blossom and rain and feathers trailing
    down?

Living in the mountains, witness to the *li* of the natural
world, East Slope embodied the mind and soil of the place
he cultivated.

Imagine for a moment that you are on a journey of
discovery, one of the lucky travelers to hike deep into
the remote Shui-hsu Valley, near the northeast border
of Sichuan providence, not far from the home soil of
East Slope. In the year 1943, Wang Zhan, a young forester from the Central Forestry Experiment Institute,
on such a journey to the botanically diverse forest of
Shennongjia, was forced to stop for rest and recovery—
he had contracted malaria—in the village of Wanxian.
A former fellow student, now the principal of a local
agricultural college, asked Wang: "Would you be willing
to identify a most unusual tree that grows in Modaoxi, a
village not far from here? The villagers revere this tree
for its healing properties and they have built a temple
at the base of it." (One villager told a later botanical
explorer: "There must be a god in the tree.")

When Wang Zhan visited the landscape of lowland
canyons and rice fields, he was unable to recognize the
impressive tree, known by the villagers as *shui-sa*, a water
fir. He took cuttings and gathered ten stemmed cones from

the tiled roof of the temple; in his notebook he recorded the date, July 21, 1943. He returned to Chongqing with probable evidence of an undiscovered species. The Sino-Japanese War interrupted any normal flow of exchange, but a few years later he sent his collection to Zheng Wanjun, a dendrologist at the National Central University. In 1946, Zheng, also suspecting this to be evidence of a new genus or family, dispatched a graduate student to Modaoxi for further cuttings. Now with a larger collection, Zheng sent all to the Harvard-trained professor Hu Xiansu at the Fan Memorial Institute of Biology in Beijing.

Hu just happened to have at hand a certain image of a five-million-year-old fossil, photographed by a Japanese paleobotanist named Miki Shigeru. In 1941, when Miki examined the fossil, supposed to be the imprint of a sequoia tree, he noted that the leaves were opposing rather than alternate. So he named the fossil *Metasequoia* (like a sequoia/redwood). The leaves of the tree so revered in Modaoxi matched Miki's fossil.

Hu dispatched some specimens to his mentor at Harvard, Dr. E. D. Merrill, who then sent samples to Dr. Ralph Chaney, a paleobotanist at UC Berkeley. According to Milton Silverman, a reporter for the *San Francisco Chronicle* who was present at the event, when Chaney opened the packet containing tissue from a living tree—thought to have disappeared millions of years ago—he fainted!

In 1947, Harvard University's Arnold Arboretum financed an expedition of Chinese botanists to collect seeds of this living fossil, and seeds were then distributed to various institutions in the United States, Ireland, and throughout China. In 1948, while the Chinese Civil War was raging, the Save the Redwoods League sponsored an expedition, led by Chaney, who invited Silverman to come along. It was an extremely arduous journey, up the Yangtze River and deep into a remote landscape, and Chaney, who suffered from asthma, was severely ill at one point. But when he stood at the base of a magnificent *Metasequoia* in the Valley of the Tiger, he had this to say: "Here was a fossil come to life, a giant whose kind had persisted out of the past to tell us the story of the earth millions of years before man came to live on it." (I can't resist—I am a tiger as I write in the Year of the Tiger). In a paper published in 1948, Hu and Zhang named the water fir *Metasequoia glyptostroboides* because of the distinct resemblance to the Chinese swamp cypress, *Glyptostrobus pensilis*, also a deciduous conifer.

Chaney returned to California with seeds and a few seedlings, and he spent many years propagating the living fossil there in Berkeley, and dispersing plants throughout the globe. He estimated that in his lifetime over twenty-nine thousand trees were established in the United States, and in Japan over a hundred thousand *Metasequoia* found a place in new soil. Chaney personally escorted two trees to Japan and presented these as a gift to the emperor.

Among the trees that coexist with *Metasequoia*—oak, chestnut, sassafras, beech, pine, and sweet gum—the water fir is often noted to be the biggest, strongest, straightest of them all (which is perhaps less important than its healing properties). Peter Raven, president emeritus of the Missouri Botanical Garden, believes that *Metasequoia*, now commonly known as dawn redwood, was perhaps once the most abundant tree in the forests of North America—fifty million years ago, at the dawn of history.

There are many players and various versions of the discovery story of this ancient tree, but at the heart of it we can recognize a species that has endured the slings and arrows of time (and fortune), and that realization should humble us. With the revolution in China, and for thirty years following the decade of the discovery of *Metasequoia* collaborations between Chinese and Western institutions were put on hold. But in that explosive decade of the 1940s, our species reconnected with an elegant and resilient ancestor. Who can let go of a kingfisher breaking into flight along a small stream, beside a redwood, before a temple in the Valley of the Tiger, lit by the dawn?

Old master Tsung, the third-century teacher of Lu Chi, engraved on his bathtub: "Make it new, day by day, make it new." I carried his sage advice with me on a trip to China—it was part of the text of *Wen Fu* (*The Art of Writing*), as translated by Sam Hamill. From the poem entitled "The Early Motion," here is Lu Chi:

> The poet stands at the center of the universe,
> contemplating the enigma . . .
> seeing the inter-connectedness of things.

On the long flight, at an altitude of thirty-three thousand feet, I had ample time to contemplate clouds, time, mystery, and interconnection. I also had time to consider the enigma of contemporary China. What to expect? My impressions of the country derived largely from reading, media reportage, and from my respect for the deeply ecological rivers-and-mountains poetic tradition. Nearing China, I turned to my compact book of poems *Pilgrim of the Clouds*, and to the eighth-century poet Tu Fu: "The window / Frames the western mountains, white / With the snows of a thousand years."

I had been invited to attend an international conference on community-supported agriculture (CSA); we arrived in the Shunyi District of Beijing—one and a half hours from the center of the capital—prior to the conference, for two days of visits to local farms. Shunyi is located at the approach to the Yanshan mountain range, about an hour south of a portion of the Great Wall, that human stone print that zigzags for over thirteen thousand miles—extraordinary!—throughout northern China (the Ming Great Wall, the most well-preserved section, extends for fifty-five hundred miles). The conference was held in a densely populated area, a hodgepodge of shops and dwellings with greenhouses lining the wide roads for seemingly endless miles. I learned that China has a claim to 80 percent of the world's greenhouses.

As a community farmer and a conservationist for three decades, I have attended conferences in multiple cities and countries, though never in a venue to rival the plush oddity of the Sun-Town Hotspring Resort. A smartly dressed bellhop, assigned to lead me to room

6307, had no idea where to find it. We searched through a number of separate buildings—he pushed my one case in an oversize trolley over uneven stone walkways, muttering to himself, as I sleepily followed behind. We entered several dead-end hallways before stumbling upon the Lotus Club, my place of lodging. In the darkness, an impressive space needle, rising above the atrium lobby, shone with colored lights, and the club entrance, decorated in a curious waffle design, pulsated purple in the cold November air.

Attendees from twenty-eight countries converged on this place, by the invitation of Urgenci, an international network for community-supported agriculture whose mission is to strengthen the position of small-scale farmers in local food chains, and to build alliances between those who grow food and those who consume it (CSA in the United States and Canada, Teikei in Japan, AMAP in France). Urgenci first hosted an international symposium in Aubagne, France, in 2004, and since then every two years farmers and food advocates from five continents have conferenced together in another country—Portugal, South Korea, Japan, the United States (California), and Greece.

A colorful banner on display at the entrance to Sun-Town announced the conference themes—under the familiar letters CSA, the following words served as a translation of Chinese characters: *Earth Care, People Care, Fair Share, Cultural Diversity.* Shi Yan, a remarkable scholar/farmer (serving for years as vice president of Urgenci) who is largely responsible for the rapid expansion of community-supported agriculture in China, coordinated this symposium in Shunyi. It was her vision and her planning that ultimately brought together an international community and the local Chinese CSA advocates (invited here for the annual CSA-CHINA conference). Nine hundred people were in attendance, united around the "phenomenon" of rural regeneration. Shi Yan and her team had organized an impressive list of collaborators for the international symposium: Renmin University of China (the People's University) Rural Reconstruction Centre, Partnerships for Community Development, the Food and Agriculture Organization of the United Nations (FAO), International Federation of Organic Agriculture Movements (IFOAM), and the All-China Women's Federation Personnel Development Training Center, among others.

One of the core texts for a student of farming in the United States—or a practitioner!—is *Farmers of Forty Centuries*, a study of traditional farming in China penned in 1911 by American professor F. H. King, and recently translated by Shi Yan into Chinese. It was obvious that the continuous exchange of ideas and practices, in classic academic tradition, was the moving force informing this conference in Shunyi. While at work on her PhD (from Renmin University), Shi Yan spent a growing season on a CSA farm in Minnesota—to "learn to be a peasant in America," as one account states—and for over five years after her return to China, she worked tirelessly to promote sustainable, ecological agriculture through CSA. In an interview with Al Jazeera, Shi Yan observed: "Change won't be fast, but the impact is deep. CSA is not just a company or business, it's a social movement."

Throughout conversations, and in the papers presented at the conference, the word *peasant* was in constant use, often in the context of "the interaction between urban dwellers and rural peasants." The usage of the word was descriptive, not derogatory (as it often is in the United States); in fact, one speaker, a Chinese academician, urged the attendees not to forget the peasants of China. He was passionate when he claimed that, after all, Chinese peasants have changed Chinese history, and that cities are really places for peasants to gather.

When I was asked by Urgenci's director to collaborate on a closing pledge for the conference, a number of us—from various countries—debated, for the sake of accuracy, which English word to select: *peasant* or *farmer*? For many countries, *peasant* is the logical and appropriate choice; the word defines a historical reality, a social compact born out of land-use practices, and, ultimately, the land. Through Via Campesina, an international peasant movement whose principal objective is to develop solidarity within the diversity of small-farmer organizations, key issues were on the table in China—agroecology as the cornerstone of food sovereignty, and the rights of peasants at work in rural areas (a resolution proposed by the United Nations Human Rights Council). Elizabeth Henderson, a social activist who farmed in upstate New York for many years (and who was the honorary president of Urgenci at the time) learned at this conference that the French Federation of Peasants had been working for years to resurrect the meaning of this resonant word. The sister to CSA is known in France as AMAP: the Association for the Maintenance of Peasant Agriculture; the name is not only honorific but pragmatic and descriptive.

My *Oxford English Dictionary* defines a peasant as "a countryman, rustic, a worker on the land," whereas my Random House (American English) dictionary offers this: "one of a class of persons of inferior social rank . . . a rude, unsophisticated, usually uneducated person of little financial means" (not exactly encouragement to youth, or to one unlucky enough to be raised in the country). In China, as in other nations, the word *peasant* does not necessarily describe a heathen, or a second-class citizen. In an address at the conference, Professor Wen Tiejun observed that, "in the course of building its identity, rural Chinese civilization must stand on this principle: . . . we must follow a path that starts from the bottom and that stresses deep mobilization of the grassroots people." Ultimately what matters in my mind is the attitude of a people in relation to the land. Considering questions of identity, ethics, and stewardship, ecologist and Indigenous rights leader Dennis Martinez rejects the common (Western) term *management* in favor of what workers on the land prefer: *land care* or *caregiving*. He uses the term *indigeneity* (inclusive of peasants and pastoralists) when discussing the 650 million or more people worldwide who may be considered Indigenous.

CSA in China has also been named social sustainable agriculture, and as such it is integral to the revival of rural regeneration (or New Rural Reconstruction— NRR), in concert with farmer-run cooperatives. In the

1920s and 1930s, a program called Rural Reconstruction
was created to bring relief to the countryside in a time
of rapid economic growth. The Chinese have always
been intensely aware of the broader implications caused
by the loss of traditional village/community culture.
Within the NRR movement, CSA is viewed as a way
to revive socially and economically depressed rural areas, and to heal the rift between urban and rural dwellers, the rift between producer and consumer. Many in
China speak of this widening gap as a crisis of trust.
The NRR may be a way to revive rural culture as the
foundation of "ecological civilization"—words chosen
in 2007 as a guiding principle by the National Congress
of the Chinese Communist Party (CCP). A village/
community of smallholders, it is hoped, will offer some
stability in an era of global crisis that threatens both
the economy and the environment. Professor Wen spoke
of the advantages of the village/community social system, which has always been underestimated, sometimes
forgotten, despite a record of over six thousand years
of sustainable, ecological agriculture. Professor Zhang
Heqing noted that more than eight hundred million
Chinese people (more than two times the population of
the United States) still earn their living as smallholders:
"The most important raison d'être of China is its smallholders." Zhang advised: "Guard a community; build
networks of support between communities." As a viable
alternative to the crisis of trust, one CSA farmer noted:
"CSA is about relationship . . . We provide vegetables,
chicken, and trust, the trust between consumers and
producers."

In between lectures and charged conversations, in search of reliable bearings, I returned to my room in Building #6, the Lotus Club, and to my notebook, to *Wen Fu*, and to the wilderness poetry of ancient China. "But if you mount the source of heaven and earth and the ten thousand changes, if you ride the six seasons of ch'i in their endless dispute, then you travel the inexhaustible, depending on nothing at all. A man of such integrity ranges far and wide through the ten thousand things, mingling with them into one vast embrace of change" (from *Chuang Tzu*). On the art of writing, Lu Chi advises: "Only after looking and listening closely can one make [these] various subtleties work their magic."

I was invited to appear on a panel to discuss biodiversity, alongside a French farmer, a Japanese researcher, and a Chinese professor from the Center for Chinese Agricultural Policy at the Chinese Academy of Sciences. It was humbling to speak of sustainable agriculture in a country that has practiced just that for over six thousand years. Perhaps poetry could inspire a leap, a meeting of East and West, so I read a poem I had written—as snow descended in the cold of November—to begin a discussion of biodiversity:

Cerulean

A quick breath above winter grains:
the sharp-shinned hawk
dives from a locust post

to glide over rye and oats.
Roots of umbellifera
reach into cool clay.

Against the dry hedge
of wild berry vines and bittersweet
the cerulean flash of a bluebird.

This landscape is crisp within earth's spin:
not the woven story of leaves,
but the bass note of bark.

In boxed hives and hollows
Apis mellifera survive
on the nectar of aster and goldenrod—

transformed and capped in waxen cells,
food for the queen of inscape,
part of the golden language of renewal.

The sun's breath above winter grains
lights the hawk's wings, and yes,
the wings of workers within the hive.

Rye survives the season of frosts
and sky takes on the color of a bluebird.

The following day, nearing the close of the conference, as I sat listening to a presenter, I felt a tap on my shoulder. A Canadian, Colin, one of the conference planners, who had worked in China for several years, whispered, "They would like to see you downstairs."

"*Who* would like to see me downstairs?" I questioned.

"I don't know. I just received a call."

Given that this was my maiden visit to China, my impulse was to question again: "Is this a common request? What is this *about*?"

"I really don't know," Colin offered, "but I will go with you if you would like?"

I didn't search for my answer. A book I had published the previous year, *Seedtime*, widely distributed, had praised the work of the Chinese artist/activist Ai Weiwei. In my discussion of Ai's powerful exhibit of sunflower seeds at the Tate Modern in London (I spent hours viewing it in the same year of his imprisonment, 2011), I wrote: "Weiwei's seeds, evocative of the oppressive power of the state, also speak of the promise of human hands, able to fire and paint a husk of clay or to place a seed into fertile soil." I never thought to disguise my sympathies, nor had I anticipated a trip to China. Was it wise to have given a copy to the Chinese professor seated beside me on the biodiversity panel when she spoke excitedly of a translation? My apprehension may have been heightened by Sam Hamill's preface to *Wen Fu*: "In our time, it is all but impossible to imagine putting one's life in jeopardy over a poem or essay, but to the classical Chinese poet, it was a daily reality unless one was willing to play cosy with the ruling class."

We descended to the lobby of the conference hall to find it empty. My nervousness increased as we each scanned the various directions for a positive sign. A door—leading to the auditorium, or the unknown—opened, and we were motioned to enter. The expansive room was virtually empty, though a studious woman seated before a computer asked me to sit down. My thought: the scene is improving.

During the biodiversity workshop, although we had not met, Jing had been in the audience; she listened, and she admired my poem. Now she needed a collaborator. She said, "I have been asked to translate a traditional song for the closing ceremony—Chinese characters will appear on screen left, and we would like English to appear on screen right. Will you help to translate?"

I am sure that the surprise and depth of my sigh were audible. "I would be honored," I replied, and to myself, *To translate a thousand poems!*

We worked together, with the help of an experienced translator, and with a copy of the song on the table—"In the season of Grain Rain / The plow slowly rakes soil." After our initial collaboration (and friendship) I retired to search for a quiet spot to continue. Solitude was elusive in such a place. As I set about the translation—

> Spring comes, full of blossoms;
> In the essence of thick green
> The cuckoo sings

—one after another, Chinese attendees sat beside me on the floor, to be photographed by a companion. A security guard offered me a chair for comfort. I accepted the role of visiting public poet, and resumed: "Quick, quick, as rain falls / Remember your rake! Today peasants sow the seed."

We were given a book upon arrival at Sun-Town published by a conference sponsor, Partnerships for Community Development: *Touching the Heart Taking Root*. Amid stories of CSA in Hong Kong, Taiwan, and mainland China, various authors take up the theme of rural regeneration. The founder of Hope Farmers' Market, Chen Meng-kai, uses the term *nong-xue* to describe the transformative partnership forged by farmers, scholars, and students in support of rural regeneration. He defines the core of this principle: "to abide by the laws of nature and to return to nature." *Nong* is "to touch the space between," *sang* "to produce," and *wood* "to live": "When roots grow from *nong*, life thrives."

In a moving finale to the conference, young farmers from all over the vast motherland each poured a sample of their local earth—transported to Beijing—into a long glass tube, as music swelled in the resonant wooden hall, one thousand people in attendance. Full of soil, the tube resembled a timeline: multiple shades of red, brown, yellow, and gold soil symbolic of centuries of earth care. The Chinese people first domesticated wild rice over six thousand years ago.

Farmers from five continents read from Urgenci's common pledge—shared beliefs in the principles of agroecology, food sovereignty, biodiversity, and the solidarity economy. The room was alive with discourse and the arts. An athletic calligrapher moved at a qigong pace with grace across the stage, drawing characters onto a long banner. A troupe of singers celebrated spring, their voices miming the cuckoo's call in flight over awakened fields.

I returned from China with garlic from Shi Yan's Shared Harvest CSA; with winter wheat, a gift from Rupert of Wales; and a long white scarf (cloud symbol) presented to me by several visitors from the Tibetan Plateau. They bowed and called me their "main cloud." This was their first journey to Beijing as well, from their ancestral lands, where "they still follow the original practice, and guard the holy snow-capped mountains and grasslands of Qinghai Hainan." They also gifted me a delicate folded package containing some thin, rough seeds inscribed with a handsome word, in Chinese characters and in English: *cosmos*. In my palm they placed a large seed head with the texture of cotton, firm in its roundness, filling my hand. Now, as I write, I pause to hold this expression of a flower in my palm, to remind me of a land thousands of miles distant, across an ocean of histories. The aroma is subtle and pleasing, and I can almost taste the sweetest gift of the Tibetan travelers: honey. Lu Chi imagines the moment thus:

Luminous words are brought down
Like a bird on an arrow string
Shot from passing clouds

. . .

Heaven and Earth are trapped in visible form.

And we travel between them, taking note of *li*, select-
ing words day by day, searching for the inner pattern to
make it new.

Chapter 5

OLDER THAN THOUGHT

... the hurl and gliding
  Rebuffed the big wind. My heart in hiding
Stirred for a bird,—the achieve of, the mastery of the thing!
        —GERARD MANLEY HOPKINS, "THE WINDHOVER"

I am no more indifferent or ill-disposed to life than death is;
I would fain accept it all completely as the soil does;
...
I must begin with these stones as the world began.
        —HUGH MACDIARMID, "ON A RAISED BEACH"

K nown in England, warily by some, as the West
Country, and as Belerion by the Romans,
Cornwall is a place where the old friendship
of stone and man is palpable, visible everywhere. The
most visible stone—sometimes labeled as Cyclopean—is
granite, and much of the rugged coastline is defined by
outcroppings of it, and by the caves carved into it by the
surging sea. This rock, in a molten state, welled up in
the Carboniferous period, and the face of the rock—
large crystals of quartz, feldspar, and mica—became
exposed over centuries. Slates and shales, known locally
as *killas*, a product of the earlier Devonian period, add
variety to the flow of the land, and a subvolcanic rock

with a handsome name, blue elvan, surfaces along the coast between the bold granite sculptures. The interaction between these various rocks led to the formation of metalliferous ore deposits—copper and tin, among others—and thus Cornwall, thousands of years ago, became known as a source of metals. Whether this is factual or not, when walking above the strong sea on the dramatic coast path, it is fanciful to imagine Phoenician merchants in search of tin guiding their primitive crafts toward the rocky coast of Cornwall over three thousand years ago.

The surrealist painter and writer Ithell Colquhoun issued a warning: "West Penwith is granite, one of the oldest rocks, a byword for hardness, endurance, inflexibility. That is the fundamental fact about Cornwall's westernmost hundred, and, unless you like granite, you will not find happiness there." That same granite, hauled, piled, and artfully placed to build stone walls, has long served as a kind of terracing on this steep and uneven terrain, so the land could be transformed into individual meadows to be worked by hardy, adept gardeners (with mountain goat pedigree). Throughout the county, the old trackways, often wide enough for only one vehicle, are lined with stone walls, some stacked so high as to create a tunnel effect. The surfaces of these stone hedges are made up of riotous vines and greenery, but the plant life only obscures the careful stone hedging that serves as fencing for the patchwork of farm fields. The prominent standing stones that appear everywhere—menhirs, quoits (chamber tombs), stone circles—in greater concentration than anywhere else in the British Isles, reflect the strong character of the place, and add more than a bit of mystery. Colquhoun refers to these keepers of ancient power as The Living Stones. Her book of that title, first published in 1957, begins with an epigram from the "Song of Amergin": "Who but I can unfold the secrets of the unhewn dolmen?" The words of the New Hampshire author Howard Mansfield read as a kind of echo of the landscape of Cornwall: "In ancient belief, stones were the bones of the earth. Stones were animate. We are, at heart, ancients."

D. H. Lawrence found a place of inspiration on the Penwith Peninsula, near Zennor, on the Atlantic coast, of which he wrote: "It is old, Celtic . . . It is not England. It is bare and dark and elemental, Tristan's land." Some recent research has uncovered another layer to add to Lawrence's observation: what is now Cornwall and south Devon, as evidenced by Earth's molten mantle, was originally part of mainland Europe. In a study published in the journal *Nature Communications*, a group of geologists from the University of Plymouth—located on the county border of Cornwall and Devon—conducted chemical tests on surface magma that welled up from one hundred kilometers deep. A clear geological boundary separates the West Country from the rest of the UK, according to Arjan Dijkstra, at the time a lecturer in igneous petrology at Plymouth.

Present-day Britain was formed from three separate landmasses more than three hundred million years ago. Originally the northernmost mass, Laurentia, collided with Avalonia; then, over millions of years, Armorica moved up from the south to fuse with Avalonia. The new theory suggests that this second collision, or a series of them, occurred not beneath the English Channel but farther north, providing the geological foundation of what is now Cornwall. The

Plymouth geologists propose that this region of the great isle of Britain located south of Camelford and the Exe Estuary was once part of mainland Europe. A geological/historical joke in an era dominated by Brexit? According to Dijkstra, "the roots of these rocks are French to the minutest detail." (Perhaps King Lear is not so mad in his madness when he questions in act 4: "Am I in France?")

Stone is visible everywhere in the West Country; trees are not. Though multiple species—including some sturdy and noble individuals—grow and even flourish in the milder temperatures of Cornwall, on estates and in protected woodlands, the county can claim an overall woodland cover of only 5 percent. This is a meager amount, most noticeable in West Cornwall, compared with the overall UK woodland cover of nearly 12 percent. In parts of Europe the figure is much higher: 28 percent in France, and over 30 percent in Germany and Italy (though twenty-first-century estimates include commercial woodlands).

As discovered through preserved pollen, it is known that most of the UK was wooded at the end of the last ice age; by the time of the Iron Age, almost all of that cover was gone. "Mankind's mischief . . . which disturbs nature's order" (in the words of Alexander von Humboldt) is primarily responsible for deforestation, and in Cornwall man's mischief was significant. Centuries later, what timber remained was used for building houses and ships; over the years, massive amounts of wood stoked the fires— part of the smelting process—for the production of tin. Historically in Cornwall, as told to me by my friend Peter Perry (born and raised there), the prevailing attitude has always been, "If it grows, cut it down and burn it."

After his return to Cornwall from Newcastle with a PhD in paleomagnetism (following a MSc in micropaleontology), Pete mastered multiple occupations—tree surgeon, woodland manager, joiner/woodworker, and most recently painter of woodlands, feathers, sea, sky, and stone. One day he set out to paint at Middle Kemyel, in Penwith, between the village of Mousehole and Lamorna. Picture that patchwork of farm fields I alluded to, surrounded on all sides by granite walls, Mount's Bay and the English Channel visible to the southeast, the Atlantic not far to the north, over the moor. "The place was absolutely howling in a northwesterly near gale," Pete wrote, "with nothing but 3000 miles of ocean between the farm and the Empire State building. And yet no one, none of the generations of farmers who lived there had ever thought it might be a good idea to fence off a little bit of land and get some trees planted, even if only to break the wind!"

To the east of the county, or Upcountry as the locals call it, the Forestry Commission (created in 1919) has thought to plant some trees—in the form of coniferous plantations. True, most of the planted species are imported—but conifers grow well and fast in a county warmed by ocean currents, and sequestered carbon in the twenty-first century is a valuable resource. For those who admire the grace of native trees, these exist in emerald pockets, such as the secluded oak woods of the Helford, Fal, Fowey, and Looe estuaries. And robust individual trees are proudly preserved here and there throughout Cornwall.

One ancient native tree, the Darley Oak, still survives at Darleyford, on the edge of Bodmin Moor. The existence of this *Quercus robur* is recorded in a ledger from the year 1030. Four hundred years later, a sympathetic arborist thought to honor the oak by circling it with a stone wall. For a thousand years now, sapwood has carried liquid from roots to leaves, and leaves have gathered sunlight to power photosynthesis in chloroplasts to feed this noble oak (and to produce in excess of ten million acorns).

I happen to have met a magnificent specimen of beech not far from Bodmin, in a rambling garden near to the village of Blisland. It dwells on a hillside, towering over a hollow abundant with ivy and laurel, a short distance above a singing brook, the Waterloo, that flows with purpose to empty into the Camel. This elegant beech, with a circumference of thirty feet at the base, is surrounded by some impressive exotic trees, but only the beech is truly wedded to the Cornish landscape. One massive root, the thickness of a tree itself, rises upward from the ground to crest along the top course of a stone wall. It glistens with moss and ivy and is so woven into the stone that one has to look close-up to recognize this ecovoyager as indigenous to the tree. In search of nutrients (and as an aesthetic gesture?), the beech has embraced the stone wall and added strength, and it runs, snakelike, for ten meters, sister to slate, feeding the canopy above.

The existence of a "drowned forest" brought some attention to the West Country in 2014. A series of very powerful storms uncovered evidence of extensive forests—pine, oak, and hazel thickets—that had flourished five thousand years ago across what is now Mount's Bay. Today the wide bay separates Penwith from the Lizard Peninsula, the southernmost point of mainland Great Britain.

Though forests are rare in Cornwall, the art of hedging is an honored tradition, and out of the top course of stone hedges stunted trees sprout and lean at sharp angles, battered by the powerful, persistent winds. The way the whitethorn leans, directed by the wind, is a revealing signature of an exposed landscape. The most eccentric example of a Cornish forest, classified as a temperate rain forest (at a latitude of 50 degrees north!), is Lilliputian in character: 174 types of lichen (lichen loves moisture) grow in the Dizzard dwarf oak forest along the Atlantic coast of Cornwall. As you descend the sloping ground toward the sea, the oaks diminish and diminish in height until, at the edge of the forest, you stand among 150-year-old trees only 3 feet tall. Should you be searching for a bonsai forest, you will find it at Dizzard.

Soon after my introduction to the Penwith Peninsula, rising daily to the first light that rides the water of Mount's Bay, I wrote the following poem: "Aria in C." Our hillside cottage faced east toward the Lizard Peninsula:

Late winter wet on privet hedge
and fuchsia's red:
    the dressed white of cove wind.

East wind stirs fabric among stones,
    clothes woven by cliff stream and cold.
My eye records diffuse and difficult tones:

sea chants and chance bucklings
    of branch and cone, self-shimmer of earth change.
List, list, here within range of touch,

scents and sounds I am other to resist.
    Lute notes of moorland
        ease with night shadow into morning,

and unearth a music, that gentle light gives
    to eyes, in a play of days.

Not far from our solid wooden door inscribed with the name Love Lane Studio, which opened to a steep path leading up to the lane, the South West Coast Path continues on its meandering way westward toward Land's End. From there it rounds the promontory to hug the Atlantic coast, heading Upcountry, toward Devonshire. On the way to the Coast Path, fifty steps from the gravel entrance to Love Lane, a thick tangle of brambles disguised the gateway to the ancient cliff meadows, my daily destination. There, shovel, seeds, and chipper in hand, I would descend through a series of steep meadows to the chosen patch, to enact a ritual practiced by villagers over hundreds of years. It was there I learned to garden, in the quilt of small meadows lined with stone and profuse greenery. James Joyce spoke of the "'druid silence' of the sea" in another Celtic place, and though the legacy of Druids lingers in the air and thickets of Penwith, it is more common for the sea to speak or shout with tidal abandon. Wave sound echoes back and forth from Merlin's Rock, just off the coast, to Mousehole Cave, a whistle away. The meadows I "tealed" and planted potatoes in were a kind of fertile crust over the cave below, a granite mouth of the headland, hollowed out over centuries by the gales pounding in from the southwest. After clearing brush or spading by hand, I would scramble up the stone steps, and if the day was fair, I would walk out to the west, to follow the Coast Path.

I came to know this stretch of the narrow track between Mousehole and Lamorna well enough to travel at significant speed over undulating earth and granite rock even when the light fell and mist or darkness settled in. The path is level from the top of Raginnis Hill out to the abandoned coast guard station, where a steep descent leads the walker through the former flower meadows down to the granite outcrop known as the Crackers. These granite steps, some massive in size, also built into walls to terrace the meadows, were moved into place with the aid of impressive ingenuity and muscle. I asked my friend and garden mentor Edgar Wallis, who lived throughout his long life in Mousehole, "How were your ancestors able to lift and build with stone of such weight?" As if the answer was obvious, he replied: "They knew how to work in them days!"

In the clearing by the Crackers, where the steep meadows leveled off, I would look up for the hover of a small raptor in the coastal air, a kestrel, as I traversed the coastal ground. This was the bird, if in another incarnation, observed and noted—in ecstasy—by the poet Gerard Manley Hopkins. Familiar with his poem "The Windhover" long before I settled on the Penwith Peninsula, here I became part of the composition. I voiced Hopkins's poem as I leaped from granite rock to rock, or stopped to watch the flight of fulmars returning to nest in stone pockets within the cliffs. I remember no separation between a kestrel's wings, my human stride, the mist of Mount's Bay, the face of granite, the words of a Jesuit.

And yet there was a leap of imagination, and a tension, something wanting a name. How could we be linked in time, within a step, a second, a minute, within this particular space? In his ecstasy the poet takes on the heart of a bird:

> . . . then off, off forth on swing,
>   As a skate's heel sweeps smooth on a bow-bend:
>   the hurl and gliding
>   Rebuffed the big wind.

And the kestrel? Through the rhythmic rush of air on her wings, the beat of her heart, she achieves a metrical dance, one that translates into poetic cadence—the counterpoint of hollow bone, feathers, and currents of air.

Farther along the Coast Path to the west, in the airspace above the headland that reaches out to Land's End, an expanse of rough ground wide enough to provide a landing strip, the Penwith-born painter Peter Lanyon learned to pilot a glider, in search "for the lonely places where physical danger and challenge are met." During our time in Cornwall, I was introduced to his work by his son, Andrew Lanyon, also an inventive artist and bookmaker, author of a beautiful, rare-edition biography of his father. We became close friends through the language of the Penwith land and the escapade of raising children. Of his father, Andrew writes: "His imagination was agile, even elastic . . . He was always curious, searching, testing, teasing reactions out of people, chasing ideas, sometimes using logic."

"I got the smell of paint very early," Peter Lanyon had said, remembering how as a child, excited by the splash of thick paint on a canvas by Samuel John "Lamorna" Birch, he leaned in close to smell the bluebells. In his late teens, Peter studied with a Plymouth man, Borlase Smart, who took him to the coast to draw rocks, and advised his student: "Remember, there are thousands of tons of weight there, and the sea has been battering this for years and years. Magnificent."

Later in life, walking the granite coast, Peter would pick up a stone and some wire to assemble an object.

"Doodling—in space," he called it, a mimic of the playful antics of fulmar gulls and jackdaws flipping about above the cliffs. A landscape in perpetual flux, where things surface in a definitive way, sometimes in a shocking manner. As recorded by his son Andrew, Peter wrote that no matter where he traveled—though St. Ives was his home for most of his forty-six years—it was the magical stretch of rugged Atlantic coast between St. Just and St. Ives (an undulating distance of eight miles) that he inhabited.

Peter recognized Cornwall as an ancient landscape, carved by centuries of mining, a scarred landscape, but one where he could explore "the region of vertigo" above sea and cliff—it was the urgency of the stone face and of the sea air that fed his being and his art. Aloft in a glider, he saw "the land blowing like tossed corn in the harvest and becoming the sky." "His brush had become a divining rod held above the land," wrote Andrew. To prepare for painting, he would advise his art students to lay down and look up.

All the elements of the Penwith landscape spoke in his work—more than line or shape or surface color—all a part of the new language he would learn to paint. A language that spoke of the passage of time imbedded in a landscape, from centuries past to now. He adored high places and edges, so he took to the air.

To feel space and to paint it, sensuously—this was it!—a bodily act, not through intellect, but with a fresh eye to reveal place, to soar into language, to feel a new beat in his heart, equal to the beat that informs a kestrel's wings.

From above, he could see and sense the energetic shapes that tell the story, shapes that remain obscure

to the observer on the earth. The voice of the land—
grass, bracken, gorse, stone, the gestures of hedges and
windblown trees that find form in the painter's eye who
rides within the sky, a sky that surrounds the pilot of a
glider. I knew this landscape, intimately, with my feet
planted on rock or soil, but Peter, chasing ideas and
images, knew it from above. Flight may be a form of
escape, though it is also a chance for a human to see
what a kestrel sees, and to capture that—or set it free—
in paint.

The narrow peninsula of Penwith—a quilt of ancient
Cornish fields, seen from above and crisscrossed by
granite hedges (some dating back twenty-five hundred
years)—is an abstraction (made up of figures), a map of
texture and color afloat in water. This is what the kestrel
sees: an incandescence of fluid matter. As the painter
glides over the earth, and returns to it, he is witness to a
wild language of granite and bramble and twisted trees,
of green, gold, vermillion, and "blue-bleak embers"
forming into words.

In a studio garden perched above the St. Ives harbor, a
kind of green oasis contained within tall granite walls
above the narrow stone streets, Barbara Hepworth
sculpted expressive forms out of stone, wood, and wire.
She was equally inspired by landscape and the human
figure, the relation of one to the other, whether the

earthen forms of Cornwall, Italy, Greece, or her birth-place, Yorkshire. She spoke of the inner beauty of those northern hills:

> Above all there was the sensation of moving physi-cally over the contours of fullnesses and concavities, through hollows and over peaks—feeling, touching, seeing, through mind and hand and eye. The sensa-tion has never left me. I, the sculptor, am the land-scape. I am the form and I am the hollow.

Penwith—rightly spoken of as a pagan landscape—was above all a place of discovery; here she developed the range of her ideas on the relation of landscape to the human figure.

Though I lived on the bay side of the Penwith Peninsula, I worked for a time in St. Ives, a harbor town that faces the Atlantic, and at midday I was always drawn to Hepworth's garden. There, though within a cultivated space and stone carefully carved, the wildness of cliffs, moorland, and sea was a strong presence—a living dialogue between art and nature. "No sculpture really lives until it goes back to the landscape, the trees, air, and clouds," she said. Her work is alive with the essence of Penwith, as the titles of her sculpted pieces signify: *Wave, Nesting Stones, Stringed Figure (Curlew), Sea Form (Porthmear),* figures with names that rise out of stone and metal in a place defined by granite—and, for centu-ries, tin and copper mining. She sculpted from the forms she could see, what she imagined they said. She was in-spired by the poetry of Rainer Maria Rilke, who wrote in the "Ninth Duino Elegy": "Here is the time for the sayable, here is its homeland."

Hepworth came to Cornwall in 1939, and later lived and worked at Trewyn, a stone nest above the tightly packed granite cottages that climb up from the St. Ives harbor beach. She praised organic forms, common things part of the soil, part of the rhythm of the land: "I could write a book about the crystal and the potato." I imagine her in sympathy with the words of the Scottish poet Hugh MacDiarmid— one who walks the Cornish moors and breaks apart a piece of rock, he mused, will find within the smell of honey.

In Hepworth's studio garden, a spell is cast by flat stone, curved stone, stone strung with steel wire, water falling over rock, branches heavy with leaves wearing a coat of sea mist. The sculptor heard music in stone, sound woven through granite and the swing of mallet and chisel, the resonance of rain that plucks a steel string. Single notes rise from leaf and stone, steel, glass, wind, my pen and paper. The language of the garden is one moment rough, the next refined, revealed in a work of bronze shaped as an ear or as a mouth:

What I hear in the garden
is visible as petals and metal.
Branch, bronze, and mist
meet in my ear's spiral.

Her aural shape is also instrument:
what wind reveals to steel and bronze
metal shapes to waterfall.

What I hear in the garden—
    rain on bone and petals—
        articulates the invisible.

Cherry flakes slip through air
    to blanket water in Barbara's garden.
        Mahogany and strings, blackbirds' feathers

cradle sound as the sculptor
    mothers her mallet.
        Her chisel sweeps through space, and stone sings.

What we hear in the garden
    is her music of forms—
        fruit of the salt air.

MacDiarmid wrote (in "On a Raised Beach"): "The inward gates of a bird are always open." She knows not how to close them, and this is the secret of her song. The Scottish poet touches stone—in his home landscape—and says he knows little of it, but he knows the gates of stone are open too: "Always open, far longer open, than any bird's can be."

I am a seedsman descending stone steps with shovel and packets in hand, to work the land. I am the walker within the space the windhover knows by the beat of her heart and wings. I am the traveler who sees the land become the sky, the listener in the garden to the music "told lovelier, more dangerous." I am the one who hears in the sweep of air between chisel and stone the elemental music of a homeland, a language audible and visible. I am feldspar and mica that mirror the glider's wings.

Chapter 6

CULTURA

with what eyes?

—SAPPHO, *SAPPHO: A GARLAND*

Yesterday goes forth from this moment, and today comes forth from this place.

—EIHEI DŌGEN

Every plant is the keeper of a story, or rather a multitude of stories, and we are entwined with the circle of narratives, as we are with the living force in taproot, sapwood, cambium, leaf, and fruit. One thread (hyphae, mycelium, or leaf vein) of a story leads to another—follow a thread and you may be led to a place of origin. Such as Eden perhaps.

When we entered the Core building at the Eden Project, we were greeted by a massive cone-shaped object pocked with numerous openings—eyes, mouths, volcanic spouts? When the mysterious, dominant object—over twenty feet tall—puffed out rings of vapor—unpredictably, spontaneously, from here and there and there, filling the hall—the question remained unanswered. We had the best of tour guides, Tim Smit, the creative thinker responsible for this unlikely enterprise—the world's largest conservatory housed in an abandoned clay pit in Cornwall. He was slow to give an answer (cheeky, the English would say), and the message of his impish grin, spontaneous, joyful, shines throughout the garden biomes and pathways of Eden.

Infinity Blue, the very visible twenty-ton ceramic sculpture that greeted us, is part of a permanent exhibition in the Core building titled *Invisible Worlds*. As Tim eventually explained, *Blue* is an artful model of cyanobacteria, a life-form that evolved about three billion years ago and changed forever the trajectory of life on earth. Cyanobacteria, once known as blue-green algae, learned the trick of photosynthesis long before plants arrived. These single-celled ancient life-forms draw their energy from the sun, and after a multiple-stage process release their metabolic waste, oxygen, into Earth's atmosphere (enacted with humor by *Infinity Blue*: as vortex cannons fired the vapor rings, my impulse was to leap and capture). As cyanobacteria multiplied, more and more oxygen poured into a world that had previously functioned without it. A few years later—about a billion and half to be more precise—oxygen levels had increased sufficiently so as to support animal life. In the revised design of the tree of life, bacteria are classified as prokaryotes (from the Greek, "before kernel or nut"), living cells without a nucleus. As I referenced in the first chapter, *Homo sapiens* are classified as eukaryotes (from the Greek, "good kernel"), along with all living organisms whose cells contain a nucleus. In his book *The Tangled Tree*, David Quammen comments: "We are, at the most basic level of classification, eukaryotes. So are amoebae. So are yeasts. So are jellyfish, sea cucumbers, the little parasites that cause

malaria, and rhododendrons." In his encyclopedic book
The Tree, Colin Tudge offers a hopeful message: "Over
the past two billion or so years the eukaryotic cell, in-
nately cooperative, has proved to be one of nature's
most successful and versatile creations. There could be
no clearer demonstration that cooperation is at least as
much a part of nature's order as is competition." The
prokaryotes paved the way for us, they outnumber us
by an incalculable degree, and they have not changed
significantly in billions of years.

Infinity Blue is placed in the entrance hall for a purpose: to remind us that our ancestral lineage on earth is
complex (from single-cell beginnings), and it is about time
that collectively we recognize the microbial players who
preceded us, who surround us, and who live within us.
Perhaps we can learn from Duke Senior in *As You Like It*,
who prefers to make peace with the elements, that which
is other. He wisely responds to the "churlish chiding of
the winter's wind": "This is no flattery: these are counsel-
lors / That feelingly persuade me what I am."

The location of Eden may seem unlikely, or random, though in fact the choice of place is integral to the
stated mission: "There is a planetary emergency. Only
by deepening our collective understanding of the interconnection between all living things and seeing them as
a whole can we protect the Earth and engender environmental harmony and social equity." The design of Eden
can be traced back to a sketch on a napkin, now framed
and in place on the wall outside of Tim's office, in the spacious and vibrant headquarters of the charity (as a nonprofit is called in the UK), in Bodelva, North Cornwall.

The founders chose to build the vast greenhouses, biomes that host an impressive diversity of plant life from around the globe, in Cornwall's Clay Country, a man-made land-scape (some say moonscape) of open-pit mines and white mountains of waste deposits generated by the clay indus-try. The entire complex is built within a clay pit sixty meters deep and fifteen meters below the water table. The stark early poetry of Jack Clemo, raised in nearby St. Austell as the son of a clay-kiln worker, describes the landscape mood. From "The Clay-Tip Worker":

> Our clay-dumps are converging on the land.
> Each day a few more flowers are killed,
> A few more mossy hollows filled
> With gravel . . .   This sand-dump's base now
>   licks a hedge
> Whose snaky bramble-growths will bear
> No flowers or fruit again; a few more days
> And they'll be buried 'neath the wedge
> Of settling gravel.

A granite backbone runs from Dartmoor, in the east, to Land's End in the West Country, which I called home for a decade. (Though the distance from east to west is less than a hundred miles, the roads are extremely narrow, so travel in the county is timed to a snail's pace; for years I viewed North Cornwall through the window of a British Rail coach, the route from Paddington to Penzance). Break apart granite, and what remains is a very fine china clay and the gritty sands of mica and quartz. In the mid-eighteenth century, a Plymouth chemist by the name

of William Cookworthy recognized that Cornish rock, re-
duced to fine clay, was perfectly suited for the production
of porcelain. The Chinese perfected the art of porcelain
making over a thousand years ago, and by Cookworthy's
time, due to a gradual advance of goods and knowledge
along the Silk Road, the secret had reached the West. The
market for hard white porcelain—the purest of pottery—
was poised and ready. Years later, another market would
surpass that of the porcelain trade, thanks to the discovery that clay added to wood pulp would increase the heft
of white paper. So centuries of mining Cornish rock created artificial mountains: Clay Country. Bernard Leach,
known as the father of British studio pottery, wrote in his
classic *A Potter's Book* that "the great white conical heaps
to be seen in Cornwall, erroneously thought to be china
clay, are actually composed of refuse—quartz, mica, and
fragments of undecomposed feldspar." China clay as a resource feeds both industry and artisan craft; the products
I most respect and cherish come in the shape of bowls and
plates and cups (formed on the wheel by potter friends in
Cornwall) I hold in my hands daily.

Given the title of this chapter, it is appropriate to add
a note about Bernard Leach, the craftsman, writer, and
teacher who bridged the East-West divide in his life and
art, and who, for me, embodied the spirit of the Cornish
landscape. He was raised partially in Hong Kong and
Japan, and with his friend Shōji Hamada founded the
Leach Pottery in St. Ives in 1920. The Leach Pottery continues today, as a working studio and as a museum, but,
more importantly, Leach's influence is suffused throughout the county (especially in Penwith) in potteries kept

alive by generations of his students and comrades in the arts. He praised the quality of china clay:

> The natural decomposition of granite frees the feldspar of its alkaline content and the resulting china clay, or kaolin, is found in enormous deposits in various parts of the world, especially in Cornwall. This primary clay is found near its mother rock. It is an invaluable material for potters because it withstands very high temperatures while retaining its colour.

The journey to Eden for Tim Smit actually began not far away, at a place called Heligan, a valley inland from the port of Mevagissey, when, on hands and knees with the heir of the Heligan property, John Willis, he crawled, cut, and climbed his way through an under-world of tangled hedges, thick brambles, massive laurel trunks, and thickets of bamboo. What they discovered was the overgrown ornamental gardens of the Tremayne family estate, once maintained by a staff of twenty-two gardeners. Seventy years of unchecked ivy, vines, fallen branches, and trees made the place almost impenetrable, and impossible to inventory. On the day that the explorers found the Thunderbox Room (the loo, or privy), and the signatures on the dark, damp plaster of those who had labored at Heligan, they were moved to restore the garden, but not "by putting it in aspic." As Tim writes in *The Lost Gardens of Heligan*:

> We had flesh and blood in mind. We wanted to hold a mirror up to the past and tell the story of these people, in a way we hoped they would have understood and approved of . . . to celebrate the lives of all those ordinary men and women who had once worked in great gardens like these. It would be a completely new way of telling an old story.

Introduced to Heligan by Tim, one of its founding explorers, I was keenly aware of that legacy everywhere—in the walled vegetable garden, the flowing mountains of rhododendrons, the exotic ferns, the path through ancient oaks, the *Mud Maid* earthen sculpture in repose. About 350,000 people per year now visit the Lost Gardens of Heligan, and they encounter much more than a restored garden; the diversity and abundance of the plant world are on full display, and the interdependence of our species and other species is celebrated and cultivated through husbandry and art.

The old story begins circa 1780, when Squire Henry Hawkins Tremayne first laid down plans for extensive gardens. Tremayne's descendants, keen horticulturists for generations, expanded the gardens to include glasshouses, a pineapple pit (a popular experiment of the time), an Italian ornamental garden, a subtropical valley garden (the Jungle), and the largest collection of tree ferns in Britain. Tree ferns are among the oldest living plants in the world, and they are the only group of spore-bearing arborescent (treelike) plants still in existence. Native to Australia, *Dicksonia antarctica*, a traditional bush food for Aboriginal people, is an evergreen that can grow to a height of thirty feet, and a Cornishman, John Treseder, introduced these living fossils to the county in the late nineteenth century. (The first plants to reproduce by seeds—rather than spores—arrived on the scene about 360 million years ago.)

When the era of plant collecting blossomed, by the mid-1800s, a diversity of new plants was introduced into European gardens, and Cornwall's mild climate provided a welcome habitat. Plant explorers returned from Chile with *Araucaria araucana*, the monkey puzzle tree; from China with the pocket-handkerchief tree, *Davidia involucrata*; and from an island in the Yangtze River with Chusan palms, *Trachycarpus fortunei*. Sir Joseph Dalton Hooker traveled to the Himalayas and brought back Hooker rhododendrons, which flourish at Heligan more than 150 years later. The age of tragic colonial overreach was by definition also a time of discovery and observation. The natural world and our participation within it *are* complex, interconnected, and, I will say, radiant. The persistent need of our species to conquer puts us at odds with the abundance of life that surrounds us, and our refusal to act with reciprocity in mind and heart devolves to a planet in peril. After the era of exploration, we have entered an era of restoration, of the need to know and respect indigenous and diverse life-forms, and the choice to participate, rather than to dominate, is ours to make.

In this same era, three very influential European naturalists set off to explore distant landscapes and natural wonders. I use this word consciously—the word *wonder* did not elicit disdain in the nineteenth century (nor in the mid-twentieth century, at least for the early ecologist Aldo Leopold, who wrote in 1940 that scientific research should be "the creation and exercise of wonder, of respect for workmanship in nature.") Alexander von Humboldt, within his time called the most famous man in the world (after Napoleon), traveled for years throughout South America, along the Orinoco River and the Magdalena River, scaling the volcano Chimborazo, and years later to the Kazakh Steppe on Russia's Mongolian border, observing, collecting, and writing. *Voyage to the Equinoctial Regions of the New Continent* expanded to thirty-four volumes, and at age sixty-five Humboldt published his masterwork, *Cosmos: A Sketch of a Physical Description of the Universe*, based on the Greek word for beauty and order: *kosmos*. *Essay on the Geography of Plants*, the first volume of *Voyage*, was, according to his exquisite biographer Andrea Wulf, "the world's first ecological book." When Charles Darwin shipped off on the *Beagle*, he carried with him Humboldt's seven-volume *Personal Narrative of Travels to the Equinoctial Regions of the New Continent;* it was because of Humboldt's example, Darwin said, that he yearned to travel to distant lands. In 1866, the German zoologist Ernst Haeckel, following the route and footsteps of Humboldt and mesmerized by Darwin's *On the Origin of Species*, set sail for the island of Tenerife. In that same year, Haeckel coined a word to describe a new discipline, building on the work of previous naturalists: *oecologie*, or *ecology*, derived from the Greek word *oikos*, "household." The earth is our home.

After the First World War, everything—all layers of individual and collective life—"changed, changed utterly" (in Yeats's phrase), and so too the estate and gardens at Heligan suffered a long decline. When Tim Smit and

John Nelson and other intrepid gardeners hacked their way into the unplanned jungle, they too were explorers encountering a lost world. The restoration of the Lost Gardens of Heligan—the work of countless volunteers and staff and years—was inspired by the soil that received and nurtured such a diversity of plant life, and in turn nurtured those who labored there. How to name the structure within a soil that is hidden, fertile, and the source of so much mythology? Speaking of this garden rediscovered by late-twentieth-century explorers, Tim evokes what is almost inexpressible:

> As the pall of eternal slumber was lifted from her, we sensed the return of her own deep, steady pulse and found to our joy that warm blood still coursed through her veins. The more we cherished her, the more exhilarated we felt . . . We succumbed to her spell.

Eden, as the name suggests, is a living landscape; each of the massive biomes contains more than one thousand plant varieties carefully chosen and collected, a convincing argument that plants are our lifeblood, from maize to oranges and olives, coffee and rice. It is not solely the quantity of plants that is impressive but the diversity of species that flourishes in what was once a waste pit. The mission is revealed at every turn in the pathways: "the Eden Project celebrates plants and the natural world, reconnects people with them, and works to regenerate damaged landscapes."

Eden exists as a correction to the ecological dilemmas created by our species; in the words of aural historian Jack
Loeffler, "We have left our Edenic Pleistocene heritage to
pursue a different sort of destiny that now largely excludes
recognition of our place in Nature."

The Mediterranean Biome houses plants from western
Australia, South Africa, Greece, Italy, and California: bou-
gainvillea, cotton, olives, grapes, and aloe. Eden intends for
visitors to look at the world through the lens of plants,
both common and exotic species, brought to Cornwall's
Clay Country from distant places, and—to most visitors—
unknown landscapes. Among the plants:

CORK OAK, *QUERCUS SUBER*: a dominant tree in
certain landscapes of Portugal, Spain, Morocco, Algeria,
Italy, and Tunisia, used by the Romans in the fourth
century BCE. As a product, cork has been in continuous
demand for floats and buoys, bottle stoppers, flooring,
and sandal soles. Some cork oak forests have been con-
tinuously maintained for centuries, thus fostering an
impressive biodiversity—evidence of a symbiosis learned
through generations of oak and human interaction.

CHILI PEPPER, *CAPSICUM ANNUUM*: number
two on the list of most desired spices (black pepper is number one), domesticated five thousand years ago in Mexico,
dispersed and now cultivated and cherished from South
America to Africa to the Far East. Archeologists have
found that the people of Tehuacán, Mexico, consumed
wild peppers circa 7000 BCE. Agar-Uchu (or Brother
Chili) was integral to the creation myth of the Incas.
Capsaicin is the key to the heat of chili, an alkaloid compound not found in any other plant. Unlike our species,

birds seem to be immune to the heat, and they are expert at seed dispersal.

Five species and perhaps three thousand varieties of capsicum exist—Anaheim, habanero, jalapeño, poblano, banana, Scotch bonnet, serrano, to name a few types, each with multiple varieties. Because my partner in farming is a lover of peppers, I have come to know nearly every shape and contour of *Capsicum*. Pepper plants, leaf and stem and fruit, are often shimmering with color, and a compact metaphor for abundance and boldness to hold such weight in fruit.

LICORICE, *GLYCYRRHIZA GLABRA*: with a name of Greek origin—*glykys*, "sweet," *rhiza*, "root"—a plant used medicinally six thousand years ago by the Assyrians. Also called black sugar, Spanish juice, Russian licorice, and sweetwood, the plant is a legume, a member of the pea and bean family. It is widely used in Chinese herbal preparations. Glycyrrhizin, the compound found in the root, is fifty times sweeter than sugar; the plant is adaptable, and it commonly grows in both dry scrubland and moist hollows.

SAFFRON, *CROCUS SATIVUS*: a member of the iris family, Iridaceae, long used medicinally, to enhance food, and as a natural dye; considered to be the most expensive spice in the world. The red stigma of the flower, produced on a stem that rises only inches from the soil, must be picked and dried—462,000 stigmas (or thereabouts) produce a kilogram of saffron. Local legend claims that Phoenicians sailed to Cornwall thousands of years ago in search of tin, and they chose to barter saffron. Whether the legend is accurate or not, today Cornish golden saffron cakes are in demand (and remind us that the intricate flower structure of *Crocus sativus* is also delicious).

Rain forests exist on every continent, except Antarctica, and despite accounting for only 6 percent of the earth's surface are host to an astonishing half of the earth's plant and animal species. Rain forest ecology is diverse and complex, at present producing 20 percent of our planetary oxygen while regulating the earth's climate. These forests have a major influence on patterns of wind and rainfall globally. The word *biodiversity* may as well be a synonym for *rain forest*—a single acre of forest may support up to 80 species of trees. Ninety percent of fern species and 75 percent of the earth's mosses reside in rain forests. One-third of all bird species nest in the canopy, and 80 million species of insects inhabit and enrich these tropical environments. Many of our own species—perhaps 150 million at present—have evolved within this ecology: part of the biodiversity, not apart from it.

Several years ago, an in-depth study concluded that the loss of tropical forests continues to have an accelerated impact on the earth's climate. Eight percent of the world's annual carbon emissions are the result of tropical-forest clearing and burning. Intact forests store carbon on a massive scale, twice that of forests that have been disturbed by roads or logging. Living trees sequester carbon; clear-cutting releases it. Not only are rain forests the oldest living ecosystems (some forests have endured for seventy million years) but also, as we are increasingly aware, they are among the most fragile. John W. Reid and Thomas E. Lovejoy, in their *New York Times* article "The Road to

Climate Recovery Goes through the Wild Woods," point out how critical it is to protect the ways of life of forest cultures, the Indigenous people who act as forest guardians. To preserve the forest, preserve the inalienable rights of the people (the United Nations Declaration on the Rights of Indigineous Peoples, UNDRIP, was adopted in 2007). Eden offers a sobering reminder that an area of rain forest equal to the size of the Bodelva biome is destroyed every fourteen seconds (even more sobering, the seconds are ticking—when I began my research the number that Eden listed was sixteen). What does the mind do with such a raw statistic? Perhaps one way forward is to increase recognition of the diverse plant life that rain forests bring forth. As Richard Powers writes in his recent novel *Bewilderment*, "If some small but critical mass of people recovered a sense of kinship, economics would become ecology."

The Eden rainforest biome contains plants from Southeast Asia, West Africa, and tropical South America: wild banana, pitcher plant, pineapple, sugarcane, cacao, jade vine, and the baobab, known as the upside-down tree, a species long revered by the African people and a tree that will branch out in a later chapter. Among the plants:

VANILLA, *VANILLA PLANIFOLIA*: a member of one of the largest flowering plant families, the fantastic Orchidaceae, this vine can climb up to a hundred feet. The Indigenous Totonac people of Mexico cultivated this invaluable orchid over one thousand years ago. A story is told that Xanat, daughter of a fertility goddess, so loved a Totonac youth that she transformed herself into a plant— *Vanilla planifolia*—to provide pleasure and happiness for the people she loved.

To produce vanilla flavoring is labor-intensive and time-consuming, as the flower, pollinated by native bees and hummingbirds in its place of origin, must be hand-pollinated elsewhere in the world. In the traditional method, beans are laid out to dry and allowed to ferment, and finally the aromatic essence, vanillin, is extracted using ethanol. This tropical orchid is now cultivated in Mauritius, Réunion, Indonesia, and Tahiti; the world consumes 5.5 million tons of vanilla per year.

COFFEE, *COFFEA ARABICA*: This iconic plant did not reach the tropical climate of the Americas until the eighteenth century—legend claims that Kaldi, an Ethiopian herdsman, realized the aphrodisiac qualities of the plant when he witnessed the ecstasy of his goats as they fed on the leaves and berries of coffee trees (the leaves also contain caffeine). Coffee as a stimulating drink spread throughout the Arab world, and became known as "the beverage of the friends of God." It was not until the sixteenth century that foraging progressed to extensive cultivation, in Yemen. An attractive evergreen, either a shrub or small tree, each plant can produce fruit (containing seeds—beans) for fifteen to twenty years. The introduction of a single plant to the island of Martinique by the French in 1723 led to a series of plantations spreading out over Latin America; Brazil now produces one-quarter of the world's supply of coffee. With this one plant, we come face-to-face with questions that revolve around social equity and responsibility. Is it enough to promote responsibly sourced coffee? The Rainforest Alliance certifies the arabica beans served at Eden, shade-grown under diverse trees to preserve biodiversity. How to step (or sip) further and slow or reverse the destruction of habitats essential to life on earth? Eden believes that education is key to the process of recovery: "We are an educational charity and social enterprise. Our global mission is to create a movement that builds relationships between people and the natural world." Eden is presently engaged in partnerships to build future Eden projects in the north of the UK (two); Qingdao and Jizhou, China; Australia; New Zealand; and in Costa Rica.

PITCHER PLANT, *NEPENTHES SPECTABILIS X VENTRICOSA*: is a climbing herb that twines upward over fifty feet. It is carnivorous, feeding primarily on insects, though occasionally rodents may be lured into the pitcher. A hollow sac hangs at the end of a tendril, suspended from the vine, and it wears a bright collar filled with nectar-secreting glands to attract the next meal. Another name for the plant: monkey cup. When the pitcher fills with water, it serves to satisfy thirsty monkeys.

Who would expect to find such messages from the world of plants in an abused landscape, an abandoned clay pit at fifty degrees latitude on the southwest peninsular coast of Britain?

On the upper path of the Rainforest Biome, a series of murals reveals stories of the human-plant interconnection, the impulse that pervades Eden. The paintings were created by a Peruvian maestro *vegetalista*—a shamanic herbalist—Don Francisco Montes Shuna, and his artist wife, Yolanda Panduro Baneo, members of the Indigenous Amazonian Capanahua ethnic group; the art vibrates with the life of plants that are used for spiritual purification. The *shacapa* is a sacred plant used for ceremonial rattles to draw impurities from the body—a plant that absorbs energy from the eye of the universe. One mural, *Dance of the Spirits,* celebrates the abundance of vegetation that germinates, flowers, and lives to release seeds on the wind. Three trees offer healing guidance and medicinal instruction to the *vegetalistas* in the painting *The Spirit of the Grandfather Trees.* Shuna received a vision of Eden before the clay pit was hollowed out; in the painting that arose from his vision, two mountains guard a secret buried in the earth. A green star at the summit of one mountain connects to the earth; a vibrant blue star touches the sky. The wind above and the sea below offer protection, and the eyes of the world—one in the sky, one embedded in the clay and greenery of Eden—focus on healing. One more "of the earth's inexhaustible ways of seeing."

"Plants at Eden are a metaphor for working with the grain of nature," Tim Smit writes in his book *Eden.* Follow the grain of a single plant to grasp an understanding of mutuality, of the reciprocal alchemy that informs the place of a plant within an ecological system. An ecology breathes and moves and adjusts in accordance to the living and dying forms that compose an evolving fabric, and our species would be well-advised to witness and take note, and not for profit. Toward the end of the book, Tim selects three words that have served as guides for the project, and that now serve as a challenge for our species to survive with some dignity in the twenty-first century: *balance, function, empathy*. I would link those words with those chosen by Aldo Leopold, a keen observer of the North American continent nearly a century ago: *stability, integrity, beauty*. The conception and construction of the Eden Project required the commitment of so many people, so much metal and machinery and architectural ingenuity, so much thought and patience, to create a graceful presence in a damaged landscape in a provincial county, in service to the domain of plants. Eden "was built on a trust ticket . . . to build on hope."

Culture, Tim reminds us, in a passage that is dear to my hands and heart, derives from the Latin *cultura*: "tillage, cultivation, husbandry." The practice of turning the soil, tending plants, learning from plants, and embracing the relationship evolves to humility. It is time to share the health.

At the eastern end of another peninsula, 3,147 miles across the Atlantic (according to the signpost at Land's End, Cornwall), and eight degrees south, I recently discovered another Eden, this one "a cultural archive of trees dedicated to environmental storytelling." In conception, scale, and setting so different from Cornwall's Clay Country Eden, its story line rhymes in a significant way. This garden, not far from my home on the South

Fork of Long Island, is tucked into a 14-acre homestead/ farmstead in Springs, East Hampton, an accurate name for the creative human and biotic expressions that vibrate on the far reach of this fishtailed island. A long country block to the north of the Marders' pollinator garden is the studio where Jackson Pollock and Lee Krasner experimented with abstraction, a long block to the south the studio where Willem de Kooning painted for three decades at the close of the twentieth century (among those influenced by this landscape are my favorites: *Rosy-Fingered Dawn at Louse Point* and *Pastorale*). Elaine de Kooning, another master painter and a dear family friend, settled here a stone's throw away, after a long career in New York City, and she lured my mother-in-law, the abstract painter Connie Fox, to move here; Connie met and later married the gifted sculptor William King, and this book would not exist without their influence and their communication with this island place. Several of Bill's expressive, tall figures interact with the specimen trees on the Marders' property, a "delicious" friendship, to use a word Bill favored. So many artists drawn to this place primarily because of the light. Willem speaks of his late paintings: "The figures are floating, like reflections in the water. The color is influenced by the natural light. That's what is so good here." In the fields and salt marshes a few steps away, generations of Algonquians and, later, colonial settlers cultivated crops on the glacial till and harvested salt hay, bathed in the brilliant light.

Enter the gate of the Marder family compound and you are surrounded by a flurry of life: extraordinary trees, experimental gardens, heritage pigs, crested

Indian Runner ducks, biochar production, buckwheat as soil and pollinator nourishment, the lone one-legged gull that commands a central field, and the one and only Folly Tree Arboretum. Just as the biomes of Eden chorus a new story, so too does this young arboretum expand beyond the boundaries of practical, profitable, and logical. At the heart of this garden is an abstract concept, the enigmatic folly tree, a unique cultivar that does not necessarily possess commercial horticultural value. Within the abstraction, however, there is real wood (I touched branches and bark, and the witches'-broom!): 250 species of culturally significant trees that "promote an exuberant environmental ethic."

Tucker Marder, who founded the arboretum at age twenty-three, grew up on this property, surrounded by trees arriving and departing, some taking root—the original site of an organic tree nursery his parents began a few decades ago. The Marders' nursery—separate from the arboretum—now employs about a hundred people, and they are known for taking on large-scale projects and for moving very large trees. Aware of the complexity of issues clouding our relationship to the natural world, and with trees at the center of his vision, Tucker's idea is to foster creative storytelling to counter apathy and hopelessness, especially among emerging generations. A multimedia artist himself, he has recently established a residency program for artists working in any and all disciplines. The Dancing Tree Award supports innovation in the arts. The criteria for applicants invite innovation: the artist is encouraged to be risky, wacky, weird, playful, hopeful, and effective! A challenge to anything categorical or academic, yes, and to prevailing trends; I am in favor of the exuberance that will bud out from such sapwood.

Here is a sample of the trees at frolic in the Folly Tree Arboretum, most from cuttings that Tucker made of culturally significant trees:

THE MOON TREE: In 1971, on the flight of Apollo 14, astronaut Stuart Roosa, a former U.S. Forest Service smoke jumper, carried with him about four hundred tree seeds, part of a joint project between NASA and the USFS. Loblolly pine, sycamore, sweet gum, redwood, Douglas fir. How would the seeds react to travel in space, to weightlessness? Would they still embody life (as seeds do) and germinate after return to earth? Experiments are often unpredictable, by definition. The seeds circled the moon, with Roosa, and returned to the planet of their birth, though in the decontamination process the seed canister burst open! Seeds everywhere, though *home*, I suppose we could say. They survived the journey and the reentry test, and following germination many seedlings were planted out across the country to celebrate the United States' bicentennial. A sycamore cutting—several in fact—live on in Springs.

THE PEACE GINKGO: This living fossil, *Ginkgo biloba*, the maidenhair tree, is remarkable—the single species of a once-varied family to weather innumerable climatic changes, and so it has for over two hundred million years. Peter Crane, author of a brilliant biography of *Ginkgo biloba*, celebrates the tree's cambium as a "cylinder of living cells." Six ginkgos

survived the atomic blast at Hiroshima, one located less than a mile from the epicenter. Offspring and cuttings from these resilient trees—Hibaku-Jumoku—live on as symbols of endurance to spread a message of peace. Green Legacy Hiroshima has distributed cuttings of the resilient survivors to thirty-eight countries; Tucker grafted a cutting from a ginkgo planted in the Peace Garden at Yale. It is almost impossible to imagine such destruction, such waste, the result of sustained strategy (so many innovative minds), energy, and resources . . . but a single tree, a true survivor, invites us to do so, to remember.

OSAGE ORANGE: *Maclura pomifera*, named after the Osage people of Missouri, is also known as the hedge apple, *naranjo chino* (Chinese orange), and *bois d'arc* (wood of the bow). Native American bow makers were known to travel hundreds of miles to collect Osage—the wood is very hard, though flexible. The fruit, however, is key to Osage as a member of the Folly Tree Arboretum. In fact it may be the folliest, if you will allow such a word. Osage is a relative of breadfruit (*Artocarpus*), and the fruit is wonderfully strange, the size of a softball, formed like a brain, and in color a luminous green. One affectionate label: "an elephant fruit in a land without elephants." About thirteen thousand years ago, giants of the elephant clan—mammoths, mastodons, and giant ground sloths—roamed the land of North America. Over millions of years, these animals evolved with plants that provided sustenance. Then at the end of the Pleistocene, in a geological instant, many large mammals disappeared, and so too many of the plants that nourished them. But not Osage orange, *Maclura pomifera*. The Folly variety is aptly labeled "cannonball," an example of an ecological anachronism (as is the avocado, *Persea americana*), a plant that lives in a time warp, a species adapted for a lost world! Mules of the Anthropocene adore the fruit, it has been discovered, though Tucker compares the flavor to a pineapple dipped in gasoline. Hmm.

ISAAC NEWTON'S APPLE TREE: Though some are in doubt, there is convincing written evidence by several of Newton's contemporaries that Isaac had his eye on a falling apple in the garden of his birthplace, Woolsthorpe Manor, in 1666. It was there, in Lincolnshire, that he imagined the principle of universal gravitation. A fellow of the Royal Society, William Stukeley, recounted words of Newton's when they met in London:

> after dinner, the weather being warm, we went into the garden, & drank thea under the shade of some appletrees, only he, & myself. amidst other discourse, he told me, he was just in the same situation, as when formerly, the notion of gravitation came into his mind. "why should that apple always descend perpendicularly to the ground," thought he to him self: occasion'd by the fall of an apple, as he sat in a comtemplative mood: "why should it not go sideways, or upwards? but constantly to the earths centre? assuredly, the reason is, that the earth draws it. there must be a drawing power in matter. & the sum of the drawing power in the matter of the earth must be in the earths center, not in any side of the earth. therefore dos this apple fall perpendicularly, or toward the center. if matter thus draws matter; it

must be in proportion of its quantity. therefore the
apple draws the earth, as well as the earth draws
the apple."

This honored Flower of Kent was toppled by a storm
in 1816, but the fallen tree re-rooted and survives today, now over 350 years old. Tucker's specimen comes
from the Silver Creek Nurseries, Manitowoc, Wisconsin;
the nursery received a clone from a tree planted at the
University of Wisconsin–Madison, and traced it back to
Woolsthorpe Manor.

LAST LIVING JOHNNY APPLESEED TREE: One
survives, certified by the organization American Forests,
planted by John Chapman over 170 years ago in the village of Savannah, Ohio (Johnny died in 1845). Johnny
was not fond of grafting; instead he collected the seeds that
remained after the fruit was pressed for cider. The Algeo
family has tended this special *Malus domestica* for over a
century. The secret of this lone apple tree that still bears
copious fruit? Rambo, a tart cooking apple, is a tenacious
variety, and this specimen was planted directly over an
underground aquifer. Transported to Long Island and the
damp climate of the South Fork, not far from the Atlantic,
this Appleseed scion may be challenged to survive a century, though at the moment I sense some exuberance.

THE TREE OF HIPPOCRATES: The so-called father of modern medicine was born on the Greek island
of Kos in 460 BCE, and he chose to teach medicine in
the shadow of an Oriental plane tree, *Platanus orientalis*
(our sycamore). The plane tree that provided shade for
Hippocrates—twenty-one centuries ago—was replaced

about five hundred years ago, and the government of Greece presented a cutting of this descendant to the U.S. National Institutes of Health, located in Bethesda, Maryland, in 1961. When the tree was ailing, due to a common fungal disease that affects sycamores, the NIH enlisted the Archangel Ancient Tree Archive, from Copemish, Michigan, to clone the historic tree (you will be properly introduced to the AATA in a later chapter). The Tree of Hippocrates has now been replanted in Bethesda, and also in Springs. The message of the Greek physician, "Wherever the art of medicine is loved, there is also a love of humanity," is carried on by a broadleaf tree and the humans who tend it.

THE TREE THAT OWNS ITSELF: Colonel William H. Jackson, a nineteenth-century professor at the University of Georgia, provided an unusual legacy for an oak: "For and in consideration of the great love I bear this tree and the great desire I have for its protection for all time, I convey entire possession of itself and all land within eight feet of the tree on all sides." The record of his legacy did not appear until 1890, though the colonel died sometime in the 1820s; now the oak owns itself because everyone agrees to the compact (remove the concept of owner-ship and our jurisdiction regarding other living things is rather a moot point). The town of Athens, Georgia, has always honored Jackson's wish; after a windstorm felled the beloved tree in 1942, the citizens of Athens planted an acorn of the white oak in the same place, and so the off-spring of the tree that owns itself survives to leaf out each spring. The granting of personhood to species, water-sheds, and anything other than *Homo sapiens* is a much broader question. In 2017 the New Zealand government granted personhood to the Wanganui River. Preceding that, in the Te Urewera Act of 2014, a forest sacred to the Maori was declared to have standing as a legal entity. Richard Powers, in *The Overstory*, a novel that branches out of trees, introduces a character to address this issue: "Should trees have standing? . . . What can be owned and who can do the owning? What conveys a right, and why should humans, alone of all the planet, have them?"

A walk through the Folly Tree Arboretum is an awakening experience—so much diversity of leaf and branch, conifer and angiosperm ingenuity, each tree full of expression, each a storyteller. Consider the witches'-broom, an arboreal act that seems to fascinate the founder. A proliferation of shoots that manifests as a bundle of twigs or a bird's nest within the normal growth of a tree, the broom is a mutation caused by various invaders. Fungi can produce a broom, or phytoplasmas, described as "a wall-less single celled organism with an unorganized nucleus." How appropriate for a folly arboretum! Brooms are more common on conifers, though a wide variety of deciduous species also serve as hosts. If tissue from the broom is removed from a tree and propagated, a new dwarf cultivar is born, often named after the eccentric character—oops, I meant to say horticulturist—who discovered the mutation. Tucker is in the creative stage of naming a splendid broom that has formed on a Folly tree, a Hinoki cypress (*Chamaecyparis obtusa* var. *Narrator*). I favor the choice: Tucker's Fat Baby (cuttings of *Narrator* have been shipped off to the Dawes Arboretum in Newark, Ohio, and to the Royal Botanic Gardens, Kew to be pressed and archived).

As in Eden, tree species rooted in the soil of the Folly Tree Arboretum—and the stories they tell—are not preserved in aspic. Imagined as a journey through time, this grove of culturally significant trees radiates with the energy of diverse plant origins, the changing tides of the near Atlantic, the glide of osprey and eagle returning to this habitat, the exuberance of artists working here under the storied canopy: being playful, provocative, risky, irreverent, and effective. I know it well; I sift it through my hands often—the structure of this sandy loam soil of Springs carries within it twelve thousand years of history, and, walking within this archive of trees, I remember the words of the Kentuckian Wendell Berry: "In spite of all the history that we can learn or know, time is always starting from right now."

Chapter 7

A STRONG SONG

I ask the just Creator
so much refuge from Time
that a tale of mine may remain in the world
from this famous book of the ancients
and they who speak of such matters weighing their words
think of that only when they think of me.

—FERDOWSI

B rowsing among the book stalls on the quay along
the harbor in Genoa, Italy, Basil Bunting was se-
duced by a tattered book with the name *Oriental
Tales* inscribed on a newspaper cover. Incomplete,
lacking a title page, what he held in his hands was a
nineteenth-century French translation of the Persian
poet Abū ol-Qāsem Firdawsī (Ferdowsi). Ferdowsi (or
Firdosi, in Bunting's spelling), who lived circa 940–
1020, was the author of the epic poem *Shahnameh* (*The
Book of Kings*), and the only epic poet, according to
Bunting, to be spoken of in the same breath as Homer.
Fascinated by the story, Bunting absorbed the tale, as far
as it went, and then read it aloud to Ezra and Dorothy
Pound; they too were desperate to learn the ending.
Bunting's conclusion: "There seemed nothing to do but
learn Persian and read Ferdowsi, so, I undertook that."

Years later, while serving in the Royal Air Force during WWII, Bunting was sent to Iran (the former Persia) as a military interpreter. He had acquired a reading knowledge of classical Persian, though he had never heard a spoken word of the contemporary language. He likened his position to one of a visitor to England, fluent in the Chaucerian dialect, trying to converse with a twentieth-century citizen. He fell head over heels in love with Iran, and with people of the Lur and Bakhtiari tribes, and, strangely, their dialect was quite similar to his own medieval Persian.

Throughout his long lifetime, Bunting received little public notice of his writing; according to his friend Jonathan Williams, he had almost no readers in his early career. Basil Cheesman Bunting was born in 1900, in Scotswood-on-Tyne, as spring was beginning to bud, but not until *Poems: 1950* did a volume of his work reach the blossom stage; his *Collected Poems* eventually appeared in 1968. I have a tattered copy of that edition, taped together—with a fragile cover and faded image of the Northumbrian bard—that I purchased for a class at Harpur College (Binghamton University, State University of New York) fifty years ago. Bunting had "an astonishing life," writes Richard Burton, who published a thorough, insightful, wonderful biography of him in 2013: "Along the way he was a conscientious objector [in WWI], prisoner, artists' model, journalist, editor, sailor, balloon operator, interpreter, wing commander, diplomat, spy and, above all these, a poet." Burton quotes Bunting, late in life, as he ruminates about the semester he taught at Harpur College: "Binghamton was a dreadful climate

and in every way a most discouraging place. Dull, dull
students; boring faculty; continual snow—the last fall
about May 9." I confess to being one of those dull students, though perhaps preferable to those in Vancouver,
whom Bunting considered "like oxen." Would that we
could meet again—I am enlivened by decades of work in
open fields washed by the salt spray of the Atlantic!

The paucity of attention given the great poet was in
this one case my good fortune. Bunting had spent the previous fall semester teaching in Vancouver, and though a
university career was not to his liking, at seventy years
of age he needed a job. Milton Kessler, my mentor at
Harpur, offered him one, and then served as a guide and
comrade through the challenging (bleak) winter weather
of the Southern Tier. An adoring guide, I would say—for
twenty-five years following that winter/spring, Milt and
I read and reread Bunting, together, learned from the
words of the Northumbrian master, listened to Scarlatti
together, honored Bunting in our exchange of letters.

Bunting was influenced by his long friendships
(mostly as an expat) with Ezra Pound, T. S. Eliot, W. B.
Yeats, and the lesser-known Brooklynite Louis Zukofsky,
but also by memories of his homeland, which bordered
the river Tyne, and of Northumbrian folk melodies sung
to him by his nurse. (Northumbria: the people or province north of the river Humber.) Invaded by the Vikings
and the Danes, once an Anglo-Saxon kingdom, the
region is now defined by the counties Northumberland,
Durham, and Tyne and Wear. Imagine the shape
of Great Britain where it narrows to the north before
widening at the Scottish Borders, the Lake District,

Cumbria, to the west. Though Bunting spent many years abroad, he came home to the Tyne and the River Dee, to the Cheviot Hills, Hadrian's Wall, and to the Quaker meeting house at Brigflatts. In his autobiographical poem *Briggflatts*—"an autobiography, but not a record of fact"—Bunting incorporates historical figures, like Eric Bloodaxe, a Scandinavian king who was driven out of Northumbria by the Saxons advancing from the south:

> Brief words are hard to find,
> shapes to carve and discard:
> Bloodaxe, king of York,
> king of Dublin, king of Orkney.

Bloodaxe is a historical character (Bunting's note: "Those fail who try to force their destiny, like Eric"), but his place in the sonata is assured, as is the river Rawthey, "each pebble its part / for the fells' late spring" because of the overall pattern in Bunting's poetic imagination, and he always draws the parallel with music. That evening at the close of the spring semester in the cloudy Southern Tier, when Bunting read the entire *Briggflatts* in the recital hall, is as clear to me as the branches of oak, hickory, and mountain laurel that I see circling my study here in Sag Harbor. Traditionally, in Persia (now Iran) a *saqhi* would sit on an embroidered pillow and pour wine for a performing poet. The serene eleven-year-old Paula Kessler sat beside him as a *saqhi*, wearing a black velvet dress and pouring water from a glass pitcher. Lisa Kenner remembers serving in this same role for the eighty-year-old Bunting in Orono, Maine, and being carried away by his voice: "raspy, deep, purring, falling like water." Between each of the five sections of the poem, and before the short coda, Bunting paused, and, following a short silence, a recorded Scarlatti sonata filled the space of the hall. From movement IV of *Briggflatts*:

> It is time to consider how Domenico Scarlatti
> condensed so much music into so few bars
> with never a crabbed turn or congested cadence,
> never a boast or a see-here.

Before meeting the sidereal Bunting (an accurate word chosen by Jonathan Williams to describe a poet he honored), I knew nothing of the names of the Northumbrian landscape: fells, dales, becks, and burns. His choice of words indigenous to a place, words that live in the soil, like pebbles in the river Rawthey, create a music too, music that carries meaning, words spoken that first entwined with stone, mineral, stream, and grass, and then found voice. Fellside, saltings, sandstone, spuggies (little sparrows), may—the flower of the thorn, "knotty wood hard to rive, rime is crisp on the bent, commonplaces" embedded in the land north of the Humber. Words condensed reveal slowly the melodies of lark and thrush, the current of the beck, grubs on stubble, "sycamore seed twirling," a spider that "gleams like a berry."

Recently several writers have drawn attention to the "lost words," words dropped (with little or no explanation) from revised editions of standard dictionaries. The list is long, and many species with whom we share the natural world are left without a place on the page. Such words live on in print within Bunting's books, and come to fruition when read aloud, with "never a boast or a see-here," as he would say. They surface, in the ear of one who listens, as water rising through the hidden structure within a tree—through xylem formed from cambium—or like messages that slip along the mycelium network underground that connects living plants within a living soil.

In his book *Landmarks* Robert MacFarlane writes of the words absent from the contemporary edition of the *Oxford Junior Dictionary,* words "no longer felt to be relevant" to a twenty-first-century child: *acorn, ash, beech, dandelion, fern, heron, ivy, kingfisher, lark, nectar, pasture,* and *willow.* I suppose certain Oxford University Press editors would add to this list words I take at random from the poetry of Bunting: *moss, bracken, barley, husk, cuckoo, sycamore, starfish, slowworm, plowtime, honeycomb, firefly, rime.* Words I love the sound and sense of, words that draw us in closer to other species. Not so for the dictionary substitutions: *block-graph, broadband, bullet point, celebrity, cut-and-paste,* and *MP3 player.* MacFarlane comments that a language of the commons becomes increasingly rare, that we sacrifice "a kind of word magic," a quality that some words possess "to enchant our relations with nature and place." I found this language in Bunting's verse, heard it in the cadence of his speech, the melody of the Tyne rising above the cold, steady current of the Susquehanna, and the resonance, the immediacy of the images is with me still. In his Northumbrian homeland, Bunting encountered (conjured?) the right tools to instruct a young writer or reader—a mason's mallet and chisel:

Words!

Pens are too light.

Take a chisel to write.

By a twist of luck—and perhaps a touch of foresight—a page from the past recently resurfaced among papers and books that have traveled with me across the Atlantic and back, more than once. An instructive page it is—perhaps *the* instructive page—from Bunting's class, that spring semester five decades ago. Rhetoric 158—Form and Theory: Readings for Writers, Mr. Bunting. Three texts to be used for exercises throughout the semester, and a few words of explanation. Bunting chose a passage from a Nordic saga; from a fourteenth-century collection of tales from early Welsh literature, *The Mabinogion*; and the best-known song of Sappho.

In *Reading I*, excerpted from perhaps the greatest Icelandic epic, *Njal's Saga*, written circa 1280, the perfect hero and kindhearted Gunnar of Hlidarendi, against his will entangled in feuds, outlawed, a marked man, prepares to leave his homeland—for a period of at least five years— to escape retribution and likely death. With his friend Kolskegg, also outlawed, he books passage on a ship:

> When Gunnar was ready to leave he kissed them
> all goodbye, and they went out of the house with

> him. He took his spear, rested it on the ground and vaulted onto his horse and rode away with Kolskegg. As they were riding down towards Markar river, Gunnar's horse stumbled and threw him. He looked up to the hillside where his farm Hlidarendi stood, and said: How fair the hillside is. It has never seemed so beautiful to me as it does today, with the oats pale, ready for harvest, and the hay mown in the home field. So now I am going to ride back home. I will not go abroad after all.

Our assignment, throughout the term: to retell the story in various meters, to learn the craft. The craft, as Bunting knew it in his bones and synapses, had to do with the time it takes to say a syllable. You have a story and you tell it: the craft involves duration, the time it takes to speak the words. In the course of a lecture playfully entitled "Ears," delivered at Newcastle University in the UK, Bunting, brief and to the point, said: "A poet must write by ear."

Another page has survived (not to be revealed)—my novice attempt to set the Sappho fragment in choriambic meter (a prosodic foot of four syllables, the pattern being long-short-short-long). There was continuous discussion in Rhetoric 158 of meter, stress, quantity, and prosody, of verse forms commonly or traditionally in use, of order and disorder in art, and how a poetic line might possibly communicate, "since the poetry is in the sound, not in the meaning." The study of meter is centuries long and encyclopedic, and I respect it, but my sympathies most align with an observation by linguist and author Susan Brind

Morrow, who writes that ancient poets "learned meter by listening to the songs of birds."

Bunting's teaching style was relaxed and gentle, overall influenced by this predilection: "I like the common eye, cleared, maybe, and very sharp, much better than the inward one or the lens-aided dissecting eye." Or, this, perhaps the most sage advice a seasoned poet could impart to a young writer: "Take the plainest words and dodge them into the right shape."

Form and Theory also included some twentieth-century stories (he had a knack for being in the thick of it), stories of a lad from Scotswood-on-Tyne educated in Quaker schools who from the age of five held the conviction that it was his business to be a poet. He remembered his father reading to him from Wordsworth: "And I cannot have been more than eight or nine years old when it was borne in on me that the use of very simple words would get you a great deal further than trying out fancy ones." He refused military service in WWI and spent the final year of the war (as an eighteen-year-old) in the miserable conditions of Wormwood Scrubs prison as a conscientious objector. After some years in London as a music critic for *The Outlook*, he joined Ezra Pound, and later W. B. Yeats, in Rapallo, Italy. He traveled to the United States, married an American, Marion Culver (in Riverhead, on Long Island, about fifteen miles, as the heron flies, from my study here in Sag Harbor), and established what would be a lifelong literary friendship with the objectivist poet Louis Zukofsky. He lived for a time in the Canary Islands with Marion and their daughters,

Bourtai and Roudaba, and returned again to London. When Marion quit him (a rather blunt way of saying it), and moved back to the States with the children, Basil—an experienced sailor—lived for a time on his beloved *Thistle*, quite literally sailing and putting in, port to port. He managed to enlist in the Royal Air Force—despite very poor eyesight—and served as a wing commander, and subsequently as an interpreter, throughout WWII. Stationed in a city he came to adore, Esfahān, the former capital of Persia, Bunting developed a friendship with the Bakhtiari people: "a splendid race" he called them. (Following the war, the Bakhtiari, by letter, lobbied the British government to reinstate Bunting in Iran). He praised Iran—so civilized and so pleasant to be in (in wartime?)—and after his early fascination with Ferdowsi, he carried on a lifetime dialogue with classical Persian poets, translating Rudaki, Sa'dī, Ḥāfez, and the masterful Manuchehri, from whom "you could learn almost anything."

By the late 1940s, and while working for British intelligence, Bunting had established friendships with the most powerful leaders in the region—strangely, perhaps, the former teenage war objector was indispensable to the Western interests in Iran and the Levant. A story he told in class—I learned later that he was known to embellish—is etched in my memory. While working in Tehran as a correspondent for *The Times*, one day, from a distance, he witnessed an angry crowd gathered in front of the Ritz-Carlton, his residence at the time. The crowd gazed up at his room, and with raised fists chanted: "Down with Bunting!" Curious, and confident that no one would recognize him, he joined the protestors, adding his voice: "Death to Mr. Bunting!" Eventually the crowd dispersed, and the offending journalist carried on with his business.

I remember and raise my hat to the instructors and professors at the Binghamton campus, but I doubt that anyone had the worldly experience to match that story. In my mind as a young student, there was not much separation between the Venerable Baz, as he was called, and Gunnar of Hlidarendi, only a few miles and centuries. On that day in Tehran, according to Bunting, "nobody took the slightest notice of me." However, the regime in charge certainly did—the Iranian prime minister at the time, Mohammad Mosaddegh, expelled Bunting from the country in May 1952.

Bunting's poems are collected in an ordered sequence: sonatas, odes, overdrafts. He preferred the term *over-draft* to *translation*: for a minimum requirement, he said, a poem "should trim some known thought to a greater precision." In the preface to his *Collected Poems*, he named the masters from whom he had inherited the trade: "If ever I learned the trick of it, it was mostly from poets long dead whose names are obvious." (The *obvious* names for those with an interest to research: Wordsworth and Dante, Horace, Wyatt and Malherbe, Manuchehri and Ferdowsi, Villon, Whitman, Spenser—and two of Bunting's contemporaries, Ezra Pound and Louis Zukofsky.) His overdrafts were made for a purpose: "to study something," for through translation one could learn to handle words, "to get them in the right order."

Bunting's overdrafts begin with a version he drafted from the long poem *De rerum natura* (*On the Nature of Things*) composed by Lucretius in the first century BCE. I have read aloud this invocation to Venus a thousand times since first coming upon it, and should this present book have merit, I am thankful to the poets who "learned the trick of it," and took the time to set it down. I am also thankful to a fifteenth-century papal secretary Poggio Bracciolini, tenacious book hunter, who rediscovered the Lucretius manuscript, lost to the world for a thousand years. In his imaginative and erudite book *The Swerve*, Shakespearean scholar Stephen Greenblatt tells a remarkable story, and it goes roughly like this . . .

The Roman poet/philosopher Titus Lucretius Carus, who has been called a visionary recluse, was born circa 99 BCE, and he lived until circa 55 BCE; almost nothing is known of his life. His contemporary, Cicero, praised his writing, and shortly after Lucretius's death, his work influenced the classic Roman poets: Ovid, Virgil, and Horace. The one text for which he is known combines the imagination of a poet with the scientific theory of his guide and acknowledged master, the third-century BCE Greek philosopher Epicurus. The Greek word *atomos* first appears in the fifth century BCE, meaning "without parts, indivisible, or that which cannot be cut up." If you will, allow me to linger for a moment on these invisible particles, the unseen; I assure you the reasoning will surface. Although atomism may have been in existence for over two millenia, the hypothesis is very much alive in our time. In 1961, physicist Richard Feynman chose the single scientific statement that said the most with the fewest words: "All things are made of atoms." More recently, a Nobel Prize awardee, physicist Frank Wilczek, suggested an update: "All things are made of elementary particles." This is a fluid list: quarks, gluons, muons, Higgs bosons, and more to be revealed, we can be assured. Lucretius looked at fluid matter—over two thousand years ago—with a poet's eye: "So I insist that there are invisible particles of wind, since in their effects and behavior they are found to rival great rivers, whose substance is manifest."

In a strenuous poem of seventy-five hundred lines composed in dactylic hexameter, Lucretius imagines a world where things come into existence and pass away in a perpetual dance of matter. Lucretius used a variety of terms to describe atoms: "ultimate particles," matter, and my favorite, "the seeds of things." He also used three words—*inclinatio, declinatio,* and *clinamen*—that indicate a swerve. Greenblatt chose this word as his title, to express how radical was the transformation that we call the Renaissance—intellectual, moral, and social. The one surviving manuscript of Lucretius played a part in this transformation, thanks to a traveling Italian cleric, hailed by Greenblatt as "a midwife to modernity."

De rerum natura would have been copied by hand for centuries, though uncirculated, and known to exist only due to a handful of references by monastic scribes. In the fourteenth century, the poet and scholar Petrarch inspired a new generation of scholars to search for lost classics, and this led to a revival of the works of antiquity, studied by those known as humanists. Where were these neglected classics to be found? In the libraries of monasteries, often tucked away in remote regions, a challenge to locate, and once found, the ensuing challenge would be to secure access to the manuscripts. In 1417, Poggio Bracciolini, having recently lost his position as *scriptor* (one whose task is to copy manuscripts) to the pope, traveled to Germany to search for libraries still uncharted. He is now known as perhaps the greatest of the book hunters, and in the Benedictine Abbey of Fulda he found a treasure.

Any humanist, including Bracciolini, familiar with the name Titus Lucretius Carus would have assumed his actual writing to be lost forever. How remarkable then for this traveling scribe, a papal secretary without employment, to hold in his hands an artful poem of epic length composed around 50 BCE. Bracciolini arranged for a copy to be transcribed, and then asked his Florentine friend Niccolò Niccoli, known for his elegant hand, to transcribe another—more than fifty copies lettered by hand have survived from that time. Cicero may have been the first to praise the writing style of Lucretius, but once *De rerum natura* reappeared—after a thousand years of quietude—an impressive cast of writers came under the spell: Dryden, Shakespeare, Montaigne, Molière, among countless others. Thomas Jefferson kept in his library at least five Latin editions, as well as translations in English, French, and Italian. And a certain Northumbrian poet, aged twenty-seven, "to study something," found beauty and economy in the classic Latin of a philosopher-poet inspired by atoms, the "seeds of things."

When the manuscript did resurface, so much of it, penned by a pagan disciple of an ancient Greek, offended the Christian church—from the "first things," atoms, those infinite invisible particles, to the suggestion that our species should pursue pleasure and happiness and surrender the fear of death, to the claim that man is not superior to other creatures, that sexual love, "that honeyed drop of Venus' sweetness," is a natural expression of the universe we occupy, and to the most radical idea of all, that a human understanding of nature (which we are part of) can awaken wonder. I recall an apocryphal line by W. H. Auden that rhymes with the gesture of Lucretius's thought: "Find our mortal world enough."

Basil Bunting, with whom you are now acquainted, was not offended. He penned his translation of Lucretius in his youth, though later in his life, after the success of his long poem *Briggflatts*, a "sonata" by his measure, he honored Titus Lucretius Carus. In his *A Note on Briggflatts*—a piece he wrote because he was "teased so much by people who cannot be content to listen without reasoning," he offers a hint or two, reluctantly, of one poet's mind. In Bunting's brief lyrical explanation, Lucretius occupies an honored space: "Amongst philosophers I have most sympathy with Lucretius and his masters, content to explain the world an atom at a time." According to Bunting, "No poem is profound," but I say his overdraft of the hymn to Venus, she who embodies love and fertility, resonant with the music of our "deft earth," is a thing of beauty.

⚜

I am looking at Bunting over my shoulder. In my study, placed before two windows that face the rising of the sun above the oaks and pitch pines, and—at select times of year—Venus as the morning star: a four-foot-tall wooden sculpture of Bunting, inspired by a photograph of a dapper fellow in suit and tie, serious but relaxed, reflective, seated in a wicker chair somewhere in Tenerife, 1930-something. My dear friend and stepfather-in-law, the celebrated one-of-a-kind American sculptor William King, found the photo in a book review of *A Strong Song Tows Us: The Life of Basil Bunting* by Richard Burton. After his seventy years of carving and constructing in every imaginable material, this was Bill's last piece, a few months before he passed away at age ninety, and in a tender moment he revealed this sculpture, his art, as a gift. Bunting has been with me for fifty years, in one form or another, and as the stars disperse, a gentle morning light reaches his likeness, carved in balsa. By a twist of fate, I've inherited Bill's chisels, tools he cared for and carved with, making audacious art for decades. "Now the year ages," in Bunting's words, the choice is obvious, the tool is at hand. I grip a chisel, to write.

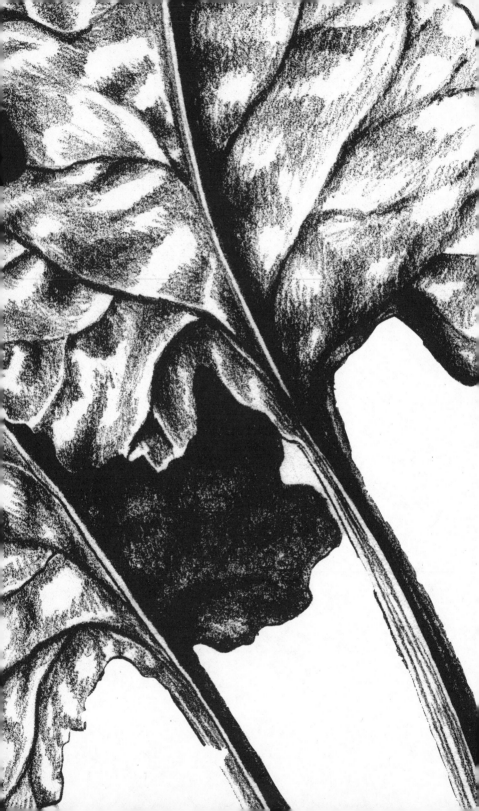

Chapter 8

JUANA'S ORANGE,
ELENA'S RED

We call this essence the spirit of life. This is what gives
the world the energy to create, procreate and becomes
the ponderous and powerful law of regeneration, the law
of the seed.

    —OREN LYONS, FAITHKEEPER OF THE ONONDAGA NATION

We assume that human beings are superior to all other
species and that we have been assured a place at the top
of the hierarchy. But it is the small things holding the
world together.

    —JOHN HAY, "A LONG VIEW OF RACHEL CARSON"

One of the earth's ways of seeing surfaces
as color on this plateau in New Mexico.
Luminous, earthy shades of red and gold
adorn both people and plants here near the pueblo of
Santa Clara (K'hapoo, constructed in the fourteenth
century by traveling bands of Anasazi): where the wild
roses grow near the water. In this kind of country, in
the words of author and journalist Tony Hillerman,
"the mountains affect the climate of the valleys, and
the climate of the soul." And here in Espanola the sky
is dominant. Air at this height has lost a quarter of its

weight—it is low in oxygen and carbon dioxide, high in hydrogen. The light is not easily diffused.

It is early evening, late September, still warm in Española, and my wife, Megan, and I have arrived at a small public park, at seven thousand feet, a place bathed in a crisp light. We are here at the invitation of Tewa Women United (TWU), an organization of Indigenous women from the northern New Mexico pueblos, united "mind, heart, and in the spirit of love for all" (wi don gi mu) for over thirty years. Tewa is a Kiowa-Tanoan language group spoken by Pueblo people mostly living in the valleys of the northern Rio Grande. In the words of TWU: "As Pueblo/Tewa women our source of strength has always been our connection to land, spirituality, and culture." Their mission and their work is embodied in the Tewa concept of *wowatsi*, to walk the middle path of balance and serenity.

We join the others, a diverse group of people aged five to seventy-five, and we climb stone steps laid into a terraced hillside, from the playing fields below toward the garden planted above. Several years ago, an eroded gravel slope was transformed and renamed the Española Healing Foods Oasis, and now the garden is maintained using traditional dryland farming techniques. There is calm in the short walk we take together, mostly in silence, each focused on the purpose of the evening: to harvest the seeds of amaranth plants.

Several visitors from Guatemala lead us to the garden, and they imbue the harvest with a festive spirit. The bright colors of their dress match the brilliance of the tall grain in the garden: ripe brushes of crimson, carmine, primrose, honey, and ocher against the blue dome that envelops

Española. These villagers from Guatemala arrived here for a short stay in May to plant the seeds with the Tewa women community, and harvest time has come. Now they have returned to instruct and to share a ritual activity practiced by the Indigenous people of Mesoamerica for centuries.

When we reach the higher ground of the garden, we surround the ripened plants—or rather, they surround us—some specimens over six feet in height, stalks leaning and falling into one another, held upright in the reddish soil of Española by mutual consent. Juana's Orange, *Amaranthus cruentus*, named after a seed saved by Juana Xitumul and Elena's Red, saved by Marcela, a Maya Kaqchikel elder, the seed hidden in her home during the long civil war that tore Guatemala apart from 1960 to 1996.

The genus *Amaranthus*, cultivated for over eight thousand years, which includes more than sixty species, is technically neither a grass nor a classic cereal grain; botanically it is different from the classic cereals—such as wheat and rice—so it is classified as a pseudocereal (as are quinoa and buckwheat). It is well-balanced in amino acids, free of gluten, extremely high in protein (the seeds contain 14 to 16 percent protein content), high in fiber, high in lysine, with generous doses of calcium, magnesium, carotenoids, and twice the iron of wheat. As a cultivar, amaranth is included in the family Amaranthaceae, a classification that now includes the previously separate Chenopodiaceae. The relationship is most obvious in the leaves of spinach, beets, and Swiss chard. The triangular, almost heart-shaped leaves of amaranth, often an attractive pattern of greens and reds, are used as a food source in many cultures. Now cultivated throughout the world—in India, China, Africa, and the South Pacific islands—and able to be grown at high elevations, amaranth may have originated in the highlands of Mesoamerica, the cordilleras. The Russian plant explorer Nikolai Vavilov labeled this region as one of the centers of origin. Each of the centers, located throughout the world, is now respected as a mother place of food biodiversity. This matters in an era defined by the loss of biodiversity; places of origin hold keys that may assist to feed growing populations. Amaranth almost disappeared as a crop widely grown, until research conducted in the 1970s by the Rodale Institute in Pennsylvania inspired a revival of interest and cultivation. The Amaranth Institute, based in Missouri, is dedicated to the preservation of the once-diverse gene pool of this highly nutritious grain.

Though the seed of this attractive, valuable plant is tiny—the size of the eye of a needle—each plant can produce as many as a hundred thousand seeds! As an organic farmer for many years, I am painfully aware of this production. Each growing year I have wrestled with a cousin of *Amaranthus cruentus*, *Amaranthus retroflexus*, affectionately known as redroot pigweed, and considered to be among the world's worst weeds. Sometimes known as one of the weeds of fertility, once this fast-growing plant discovers your fertile field, it is very difficult to control. It adores the heat and, left untended, it can grow to the size of a small tree in a month. And if one plant is allowed to mature and shatter? Those one hundred thousand seeds can live in the soil, undisturbed, for forty years. In a food plant, of course, this is a quality worthy of praise.

The name amaranth derives from a Greek word meaning "never-fading," "one that does not wither." In Mesoamerica, it was named *huautli*, "the smallest giver of life." It is at home in Nepal as well as the mountains of Guatemala, and once the plant is established, it requires very little moisture. *Amaranthus* is a resilient plant, and that quality has ensured its survival against significant odds. The Aztecs, who revered this cultivar as an invaluable food source, made statuesque figures out of a mixture of seeds and honey. Fearful of pagan ritual, and to punish the Indigenous people's reverence, the Spanish conquistadores in their madness burned the crop fields and banned the production of this staple of life (this despite the fact that the conquistadores' horses, starving after the long voyage, chose the abundant seeds of amaranth to feed on). Centuries later, this wasteful, brutal tactic was revived during the three decades of civil war.

Before she founded the Albuquerque nonprofit Garden's Edge in 2007, Sarah Montgomery journeyed to the Baja Verapaz department in Guatemala in 2002: to Rabinal, a town in the Sierra Chuacas mountains, to begin a garden project with war widows. An edge is defined as the crest of a ridge, a critical position, a meeting line of two surfaces—a place where tension is palpable. A step, a shift in time or inclination can lead to a precipice, or to a renewal. Sarah was there to assist the local Indigenous villagers, the Maya Achi, to plant the native crops that fed their ancestors—heritage corn, beans, squash, *macuy*, *chipilín*, and amaranth—and although she found it difficult to establish trust, it was listening to seed stories and honoring heritage seeds that connected Sarah with the Maya. In words spoken by an Indigenous leader from the northern territory of the Haudenosaunee, Oren Lyons, faithkeeper of the Turtle Clan of the Onondaga: The seed "is the law of life. It is the law of regeneration."

Sarah's goal was to foster food sovereignty in a people and a country that had endured unspeakable atrocity for decades. Finding a source for seeds and saving seeds became the heart of her work, and is now the work of the Qachuu Aloom Mother Earth Association—a Maya-run organization. Sarah writes: "Seeds are a place and a product and a memory; they offer us a collective inheritance in the form of a tiny and simple time capsule."

It is a small miracle—no, a great miracle—that any heritage seeds could be found in Rabinal at the start of the twenty-first century. The Maya as a culture predate the Aztecs, and have survived over five hundred years of colonization. They "have been on the receiving end of a constant offensive against [our] forms of production and social organization, culture and religion," observes Rigoberto Quemé Chay, a leader of the K'iche' (meaning "many trees") group of Mayas. Undoubtedly it is the Mayan cosmovision (the term used by Chay) that has helped to insure the survival of these people. This great civilization, which arose in time with the Christian era, developed ceremonial centers, hieroglyphic writing, astronomy, a calendar, and a recognition of the concept of zero.

The Mayan year is divided into 260 days, representative of the cycle of corn in the earth, and the cycle of a human embryo in the mother's womb. Chay writes: "Mayas believe that all nature is life: each animal, stone, and river has its own *nahual* or divine personification."

In the decades of conflict and upheaval, a few elder villagers found hiding places for what may have been their most valuable resource, placed in jars here and there, sometimes lodged under roof tiles. To begin the process of renewal, Garden's Edge worked with twelve families and a few handfuls of seeds. The mission was to collect and reintroduce traditional seed varieties, highly adaptive seeds that might revive a local culture once familiar with the farming practices we now label as agroecology. The approach is a proven one, sensible, practiced for centuries—to acknowledge and work in concert with the ecological system one is a part of. Agroecology respects the social ecology of place. It is a theme also at the heart of Pope Francis's encyclical on climate change, *Laudato Si': On Care for Our Common Home*: "We are not faced with two separate crises, one environmental and the other social, but rather with one complex crisis which is both social and environmental. Strategies for a solution demand an integrated approach to combating poverty, restoring dignity to the excluded, and at the same time protecting nature."

Closer to home for the villagers of Guatemala, the theme cries out in the sacred book of the Maya, the *Popol Vuh* (*The Book of the Dawn of Life*), where it is written that to make an enemy of the earth is to make an enemy of one's own body.

Whereas conventional systems—what dominant cultures have been exporting for decades—lead to a dependence on the use of hybrid seeds, synthetic fertilizers, herbicides, and pesticides, all costly imports, the approach of Garden's Edge is to encourage independence and resilience through regenerative agricultural practices. Through Qachuu Aloom, the villagers of the region may realize "the right of peoples, communities, and countries to define their own agricultural, pastoral, labor, fishing, food and land policies" (from the 2002 Rome Forum on Food Sovereignty).

Now over four hundred seed growers are involved in practices that foster biodiversity, instead of those that decrease it, a reversal of the legacy of colonial policy and twentieth-century industrial agriculture. Garden's Edge has initiated programs to foster seed saving through a local seed bank, to support traditional healing arts, to improve maternal health, and to install a microenterprise system to offer start-up loans. To mitigate the impact of climate change, they have helped villagers to build the first sand dam in Chixolop. Effective in Africa and also in Honduras, a sand dam will capture rainwater, conserve soil, and replenish the aquifer.

Julian Vasquez Chun, a Maya Achi, credits Qachuu Aloom for opening the door to a relearning of ancestral practices, and to creating a way to exchange with other growers. He learned to love plants in his mother's garden, and he now uses a technique known as *campesino a campesino*, "farmer to farmer," to teach other families cultivation skills, but also the less obvious values of working with plants. Through Qachuu Aloom, he has realized a dream: not only to lead in his community, but to inspire other farmers to recognize their collective inheritance. To save a seed is to pass on a story, and also to preserve an ancestral gift, a spiritual connection with mother earth. In the *Popol Vuh*, the creator is known as Heart of the Sky, Heart of the Earth, and humans were brought into being out of a plant, born of corn.

A few days prior to the gathering in Española, in a small garden beside the Albuquerque Museum, with Megan I joined university students and children, Sarah from Garden's Edge, and the Maya Achi from Qachuu Aloom to practice the art of saving the seeds of *Amaranthus cruentus*. The garden was planted to accompany an exhibit titled *Seed: Climate Change Resilience*. We knelt beside Julian to thresh and winnow the abundant, brilliantly colored amaranth plants. Julian is an amaranth ambassador in a program known as Seed Travels, founded by Garden's Edge in 2009. But Seed Travels is much more than a program; it is a way of connecting, of allowing an old way of seeing to re-emerge. Those who travel together and cultivate the plants extend the work of connecting communities in Guatemala to communities farther north. *Amaranthus cruentus*, the sacred superfood, has been planted by the Guatemalans in California at the Milagro Allegro Community Garden in Northeast Los Angeles, in Pasadena, in Bishop, and in Venice, with the Seed Library of Los Angeles; and in Arizona at the Hopi Tutskwa Permaculture Institute.

Now in Española at the Healing Foods Oasis with families from Santa Clara Pueblo, Rabinal, Albuquerque, and Española, instructed by Rosalia and Maria Elena, we snap the ripe stalks and bundle the brilliant seed heads, as many as we can carry, to transport the harvest to the lawn below. We stack the grain on several tarps and kneel before an age-old mystery: out of the tiniest of seeds placed in a substance ground down from rock over millennia, in a high, dry country, this superfood (millions of seeds) came to maturity on substantial stalks taller than our bodies. As we cup our hands around and over the flame-shaped seed heads, they shatter, and a sea of pink and gold grains flows around our knees. Perhaps we are at a threshold, the place of entrance to a dwelling. The dwelling is the soil we kneel upon as we thresh the grain, our common home; the amaranth is an entrance, our shared harvest.

When the threshing is completed and the long stalks are removed, Julian teaches a young girl the art of winnowing. She is shy, yet eager to take on an active role in the ceremony, to be in the center. He gathers the seed in a wide bowl, lifts the vessel to shoulder height, and pours it out. A gentle breeze sweeps the chaff from the small seed, carries it away, and the seed kernels by the thousands sift to another waiting bowl. Now it is the child's chance. She hesitates, unable to raise the bowl to any height; seeds and chaff fall as one, asking to be winnowed once more. Gracefully, and with care, Julian helps her to feed the air with amaranth seeds, and a mound of usable grain builds in the bowl.

More than enough seed to mix with the liquid honey warmed on a portable stove. The grain pops in the pan, and

Rosalia swirls the tiny, toasted, puffed seeds with a stream of golden honey to form a pan full of sweet, nutritious amaranth bars. As the sky color turns to rose, we taste and talk. The whole experience is an enactment of what the ethnographer Eugene Anderson names "an ecology of the heart."

Gary Paul Nabhan, ethnobotanist, writer, and farmer, in his book *Enduring Seeds: Native American Agriculture and Wild Plant Conservation*, a chapter titled "A Spirit Earthly Enough," speaks of a common thread that weaves together stories of the Pueblo people, the Maya, and the K'iche': "Their native agricultures continue today because they are persistent cultures, retaining sets of values not found in the modern marketplace." Theirs is a reciprocal practice— peoples drawn to care for soil and plants and community, *campesino a campesino.*

It is strange, impossible for me to imagine the consciousness—of the conquistadores, or of a ruling faction obsessed with power—so filled with fear of a plant, a people, to be moved to destroy every trace. I believe and I have said that our culture, our habitation in this time on earth, is in need of transformation. Here it is, expressed in the interdependence of a persistent people and an ancient grain. Here in a plant so colorful, "one that does not wither," a plant that produces seeds—in a beautiful phrase I recall from the *Chandogya Upanishad*—"smaller than a grain of rice, or a grain of barley, or a grain of mustard-seed, or a grain of canary-seed, or the kernel of a grain of canary-seed," a plant that inspires gratitude, ceremony, art, reverence, and, when warmed, wow, it can pop! Heart of the Sky, Heart of the Earth.

Chapter 9

THE REMEMBERED EARTH

Once in his life a man ought to concentrate his mind upon
the remembered earth, I believe. He ought to give himself
up to a particular landscape in his experience, to look at
it from as many angles as he can, to wonder about it, to
dwell upon it. He ought to imagine that he touches it with
his hands at every season and listens to the sounds that are
made upon it. He ought to imagine the creatures there and
all the faintest motions of the wind. He ought to recollect
the glare of noon and all the colors of the dawn and dusk.

—N. SCOTT MOMADAY, *THE WAY TO RAINY MOUNTAIN*

D usk, the swallow's hour, and a bright moon rises
in the east over the north Atlantic. The ocean
is near, I hear it, just beyond the railroad tracks
and Amagansett village—a short glide for an osprey—
though I cannot see it from my sheltered garden tucked
into the back of a Long Island farm field. I am surrounded
on every side by robust maples, white pines, an elegant
larch, a thick tangle of bittersweet, honeysuckle, and the
rampant porcelain berry, as I kneel on the sweet-smelling
earth, planting beans as the light fades. The varieties of
Phaseolus vulgaris are rare, collected by seed travelers from
distant places, and I am a willing (and joyful) conservator.
New Mexico, Tuscarora Bread, Rafioffi, Purple Stardust,

Flor de Juno "Silvia," Shinnecock. As the first star appears below the moon, fireflies rise among the grasses, flickering like earthly stars, on familiar terms with this soil. Swallows dip off toward night, and I press the last of the varietals one by one neatly into the row. This silt loam remembers the moment, as do I, as the last of the seeds, Nightfall, fills the furrow. Flash! A firefly, as the living seed too remembers the silt.

When Ernst and Katrina approached me, they were desperate. Flower growers on rented land, they had just been given two weeks to vacate their garden, perennials primarily, planted in a Sagaponack field. They had heard word of our CSA farm—a rare project at the time, a marriage of a conservation organization, the Peconic Land Trust, and a community farm—did we have space, a fallow field perhaps, a place to park the plants, if only for a growing season? I sensed they were good growers—their first concern was for the plants; *salt of the earth*, I thought, an intuition that proved to be accurate. "We've nurtured these plants from seed to flower . . . We can't abandon them now!" Ernst said.

At the time, we were bringing new fields into production, season by season as our farm membership expanded, though we had yet to cultivate a fallow field to the south that bordered the railroad tracks. "You are in luck," I replied. "There is an acre waiting for you in the back field, within listening distance to the ocean."

The lease of one acre expanded to two within a year, and our relationship, reciprocal from the start, matured with the plants. I supplied tractor work and compost; they offered labor in exchange and a more delicate horticultural understanding and practice. We learned from one another, and the example of a garden surrounded—embraced—by a farm created a firmer, fuller experience. Our annual crop fields expanded to border the garden to the north and south. Like the soil we tended and the plants we cultivated, our human connection was symbiotic, and our shared attention to this specific silt loam continued to ripen. An observation by Robin Wall Kimmerer is appropriate here: "Attention is the doorway to gratitude, the doorway to wonder, the doorway to reciprocity."

As protection from the cold north wind and the storm gusts (and salt spray) from the southwest, and for gardeners' privacy, Ernst and Katrina planted the maples and pines that now shelter the herb garden I tend. They spaded in a sapling in the southeast corner that today, forty feet in height, extends sweeping boughs to dance in the daily winds and serves as a perch for doves, red-winged blackbirds, cardinals, and the sharp-shinned hawk. This larch, *Larix laricina*, stands alone, the only one of its kind within a wide radius. Not common to Long Island, a toe into the Atlantic of Turtle Island (a name for North America, based on a creation story and in usage by some Indigenous peoples), larch is dominant in the boreal forests of Canada and Siberia. It knows how to endure, as some trees in the forests of British Columbia have done for close to two thousand years. Larch is also known as tamarack, a well-chosen Algonquian word for a Nordic species, meaning, "wood used for snowshoes." *Larix* has inspired legends elsewhere in the world: in a Siberian creation story, God first chose to make two trees, a fir and a larch, female and male. In larch forests of the Alps, it is said that kindly spirit beings sing among the old growth. They are known as the Sailigen, "the blessed ones who dwell inside mountains," kind to people and animals, a race kin to the Irish Tuatha Dé Danann. Here, so near to the Atlantic, it is the spirit from the sea that whispers through the long boughs. A lovely Greek word for *whisper* translates into English as "psithurism"—the sound of wind in the trees—and I hear it through the larch.

Though classified as a conifer—it bears very small cones, considering the bulk of the tree—it is a rare gymnosperm, a deciduous member of the Pinaceae family. When the tree begins to leaf out, the compact needle leaves form into beautiful rosettes on the stem, and in the autumn, especially on a dry year, they turn golden before falling. To my untrained eye, the spring rosettes reveal an ancient lineage—in fact, the first gymnosperms appeared on the earth 290 million years ago, so this larch has some impressive ancestry. The wood is heavy and dense and resistant to fire and water damage—it is a versatile tree. The writer Rick Bass, who lives in the epicenter of larch, the Yaak valley of Montana, and who is in love with the "odor . . . and the sight and touch of them," and even "their magnificent and rotting bodies," praises the independence of this species. I praise the independence of the one I know—sturdy and graceful, and resilient in all weathers—and its quiet dominion over this garden nestled between farm fields, herbs now thriving where potatoes had been planted for well over a hundred years. Eric Rutkow, in *American Canopy*, comments:

> Our trees are living history. Each has a story to share, though it is well guarded, locked away in eternal silence. Uncovering these hidden tales requires a degree of tenacity. One must develop a feel for the many factors that determine why any given tree arrived at a particular spot and why it subsequently survived.

I have a feel for this larch, how and why it arrived here, and I am privileged to have found friendship with the tree.

One day Ernst summoned me to witness the results of a monthlong project. He gestured at four fifty-gallon garbage bins overflowing with oddly shaped earthy tubers. Now, every farmer or gardener has a thick journal (and memory) full of stories that relate to undesired plant life—plants that somehow thrive and persist in a crop field or a garden of perennials. Dear reader, shall I speak again of my acquaintance with various invaders: nutsedge, dock, galinsoga, purslane (delicious on a plate), jimsonweed, bindweed, redroot pigweed, mile-a-minute? My *Oxford English Dictionary* lists a weed as a "herbaceous plant not valued for use or beauty, growing wild and rank . . ." The singsong effect of that phrasing would not satisfy many serious growers. Nor did the long vines—capable of growing twenty feet in a year—twirling out from those tubers impress our flower growers.

Had I known at the time the history of *Apios americana*, indigenous to this ground, our discussion would have been prolonged. Ernst and Katrina were ace gardeners, careful and attentive to a seasonal market; they made their living selling flowers, and a weed that thrived on the support of healthy cultivars must be rooted out. They were thorough, beyond imagining—they harvested two hundred gallons of groundnuts out of an acre of prime soil.

Sagaponack, a village just to the west of the farm, derives its name from *Apios americana*: land of the big ground nuts, once a staple food for the Montaukett and Shinnecock tribes. It is known by other names as well: wild bean, Indian potato, potato bean, and ground-nut, though the sweet, melodic Lenape word, *hopniss*, captures the wild spirit of *Apios* (Greek for "pear"). The Wampanoags taught early settlers how to harvest and cook groundnuts, and Henry David Thoreau wrote about his own foraging: "In case of a famine, I should soon resort to these roots." They are leguminous, in the family of peas, with attractive maroon-and-white flowers, pealike in appearance though hardier, with an acrid smell (in my humble opinion). In botanical terms, the tubers are not roots but rhizomatous stems. As with other legumes, the threads of the rhizome interact with bacteria that inhabit the soil; bacteria are adept at capturing nitrogen, and the *Apios* root-stems provide a surface where nodules can attach (known as fixation), and the overall soil health is improved. Nearby trees gladly accept nitrogen in exchange for the carbohydrates they exude in a process handsomely called mutualism (a brand of symbiosis I will discuss later). Groundnuts reproduce along the thin rhizome, "like beads on a necklace," writes Tamara Dean. Native to many soils and naturally abundant, like other tubers they sweeten as the ground turns colder.

Though quite high in protein content, 17 percent (triple that of potatoes), and rich in isoflavone genistein, an anticarcinogenic compound, *Apios* long ago fell out of favor. Attempts to introduce the tuber to Germany, France, and Ireland (during the potato famine, over a century ago) did not succeed. In the 1980s, a professor at Louisiana State University devised trials hoping to domesticate the groundnut—to increase tuber size and yield. He claimed that domestication of this "golden nugget . . . would be a benefit to mankind." After a decade of improvements and promising crops, funding slipped away, the *Apios Tribune* ceased to be published, and the dedicated professor moved on. Perhaps there is something in this humble tuber that rejects popular approval and a place in the produce section of supermarkets.

Enrique Salmón, head of the American-Indian Studies program at California State University East Bay, relates a story of the Creek Nation. An unknown band of people arrived in Creek territory, and the two groups lived in peace. Eventually members intermarried, and some confusion followed: how to include those children born into existing Creek clans? The solution required naming a new clan, to assure kinship among the people; the chosen name: White Potato (groundnut) Clan.

After Ernst and Katrina departed (for a farm of their own), this garden passed through several transformations, and changes of name. Katrina, a German by birth, was fond of garden gnomes, and a population had moved in to commune with iris and dianthus, dahlia and narcissus. The name of the garden reflected the cultivators' taste: the Gnomers' Garden. Grant H. with his beehives followed the flower growers, and *Apis mellifera* provided a title: the Bee Garden. Mary of Bees' Needs (queen of beekeepers) settled into the Bee Garden, and her hives thrived. When Mary shifted her bees to a nearby field, we expanded our Chinese medicinal plantings into the Herb Garden. Now the groundnut had a place to revive, with bees as near neighbors. Our flower growers were indeed weeders without compare, though *Apios*, native to this soil, found a way to survive (could we ask more of a traditional food source?).

Among the medicinal plants now in residence are several tree species: *Cornus officinalis* (Japanese cornelian cherry), *Eucommia ulmoides* (rubber tree), *Platycladus orientalis* (arborvitae), *Liquidambar formosana* (sweet gum), and *Zanthoxylum bungeanum* (Sichuan pepper). Wild-edibles expert Samuel Thayer observes that *Apios* doesn't "like to be alone"—the rhizomes prefer to grow alongside the roots of other plants (as imagined by Suzanne Simard, plant communication in action). And this we have learned—the base and outer bark of cherry, sweet gum, and arborvitae provide ideal support for the twining vines of *Apios*. Underground, undisturbed under the young perennial trees and among their roots, the tubers have found another kind of support; they are making a comeback. I welcome the return of the groundnut, encouraged by the interplay of our plantings and what nature interjects.

This is the story of an island soil, a piece of the earth's mantle, fertile ground, a gift of the last glacial advance and retreat, and I can track the changes over the last third of a century. I am curious what came before, but perhaps the present, in possession of the past, holds keys and seeds that open in time.

In 2003, traveling down from the Hudson Valley, Jean Giblette gifted us a handful of plants: *Mentha haplocalyx* (Chinese mint), *Schisandra chinensis* (five-flavor-fruit), *Trichosanthes kirilowii* (Chinese cucumber), *Lycium chinense* (goji berry), and *Belamcanda chinensis* (blackberry lily). Although our community-farm crop list had grown to more than five hundred varieties of vegetables and flowers, these were assuredly not on the list; a novice again, I spaded the herbs into our nurturing soil. I welcomed the chance—why not?—to join an experimental grow out of Chinese medicinal herbs. Jean had chosen us as one of five farms to test the viability of these plants in New York State. The synergy was organic—from our first spadeful of Amagansett earth, we have worked to build health in the soil and among the community that includes plants and people. Jean knew the value of our northern maritime microclimate: our long growing season is regulated by the ocean temperature— (Zone 7 on the U.S. Department of Agriculture [USDA] plant hardiness map, and Long Island is a narrow stretch of land surrounded by water, giving our fields a natural advantage over landscapes to the north [USDA Zones 4 and 5]). "Mind the gap," as the saying goes, between first and last frost, to increase your chances as a grower.

For many years, practitioners of traditional Chinese medicine (TCM) have relied on herbs imported from China, despite the fact that a majority of ornamental plants grown in North America derive from East Asia. Steven Foster, author of multiple books on the subject, created a list of 779 species of medicinal herbs flourishing in gardens and labeled as ornamentals. He shared a dream with Dr. Shiu-Ying Hu of Harvard's Arnold Arboretum that one day these healing plants would also be cultivated here in the United States. In the 1990s, in California, Peg Schafer surfaced as a pioneer in the cultivation of Asian herbs on a market scale, and within fifteen years she had experimented with growing more than 250 varieties. Jean Giblette traces her own journey to the plants also to that time, specifically her visit to Lin Sister Herb Shop in New York's Chinatown. An interest in Asian medicinal plants was indeed germinating; she recognized the seed beginning to sprout. A decade later, TCM had taken root in North America, and Jean wrote: "The phoenix is rising from the ashes, presenting a great opportunity to return to a superior model of health care. In parallel with the organic farming movement that took hold beginning in the 1970s, the profession of Acupuncture and Oriental Medicine has established itself in North America. Today over fifty accredited graduate colleges, national certification, and licensure in more than 40 states support some 20,000 practitioners in the United States alone." Jean and Peg cofounded the Medicinal Herb Consortium, a nonprofit group formed to establish connections between herb growers and practitioners.

At High Falls Gardens, in Philmont, New York, now as a grower, Jean was learning with her eyes and hands the traditional Chinese approach to healing: it rises out of the reciprocal relationship—deep in time—between plants and humans. In her thorough and informative book, *The Chinese Medicinal Herb Farm*, Peg Schafer observes: "As the global herb community faces the challenges of worldwide climate change and ecological uncertainties, as well as unsustainable levels of wild-collection, it is more imperative than ever that everyone takes a conscientious role in the conservation of these treasured medicinal plants." Recently Jean has brought together thirty New York small farms under the banner of Zai Sheng Herbs—the word means "regeneration." The goal is to market domestically grown Chinese medicinal herbs to licensed and registered East Asian medical practitioners, and to benefit growers.

The Herb Garden begins to breathe in and out with new life and new cultivars, as I now have time to care for it. Intermingled with the smaller perennial herbs— salvia, dianthus, astragalus, balloon flower *(Platycodon grandifloras)*—we've introduced several tree species, now branching out and leafing out to provide more color and cadence (and medicinal quality). In March, long before neighboring plants have given it a thought, the anthesis of *Cornus officinalis*, a tree that resembles a cherry (seed from the Arnold Arboretum), is inspiring: yellow-flowering umbels appear prior to leaves, though all neighboring plant life is bare. One of the several mimosas *(Albizia julibrissin)*, long, tropical-looking foliage that waves in the afternoon

sea breeze, flowered this year for the first time, and we harvested the delicate, aromatic, pink, brushlike flowers for
a healing tea. The deep-red-and-green, shapely leaves of
Liquidambar sing out against the evergreen leafage of arborvitae. Sichuan peppers ripen on the spikey bushes—also
for the first time this year—clusters of red beads encase the
hot pepper seed (colored black) inside.

In the center of the garden, not by
my design, a robust stalk of *Angelica
dahurica* grew to a height of seven feet.
I love the architecture of this plant,
a member of the Apiaceae family, en-
demic to the grasslands of north and central China, and vibrant in this garden. The
Apiaceae include carrots, celery, and Queen
Anne's lace, and were once known as the
Umbelliferae, a more accurate naming—the
delicate flowers, and the seeds that follow, fan
out in a globe-like fashion to form an umbrella. When in
flower, the umbels attract an astonishing diversity of pollinators, and I was witness this August to a surprise guest:
a ruby-throated hummingbird. As I knelt in the garden,
one-tenth of an ounce of beating heart and wing muscle
appeared beside me, to feed on the tubular flowers it
fancies, for seconds, only to dash to the *bai zhi* (angelica)
tree, where it hovered for a full five minutes on the flattish
white flowers. This plant was beyond desirable—though I
had never before seen a hummingbird in the Herb Garden,
now there were two. These diminutive flyers—*joyas voladoras*,
"flying jewels"—are notoriously territorial; they could not
share the nectar of the angelica, and two dark specks of

energy rocketed, in chase, into the sky. At that moment, I was reminded of two lines from the Buddhist sutra, the *Sandokai* (*The Identity of Relative and Absolute*), though I never, ever anticipated such a visual experience to clarify the metaphor: "The absolute meets the relative / Like two arrow points that meet in midair." A gift of the garden, one more of "the earth's inexhaustible ways of seeing."

It is autumn and I am harvesting the seeds of *Anemarrhena*, a plant I am strangely drawn to, despite its far-from-showy, somewhat odd appearance, and of *Scrophularia* (figwort), a compact bush that produces tiny red-brown flowers that rival angelica in attracting pollinators, especially bumblebees (five times the size of the flower). For the bee, to gather nectar requires dedication, and dexterity (of wings and abdomen). There is radical variation in the task of saving the seeds of these perennial herbs. *Anemarrhena* sends up a thin, tough flower stalk almost four feet, speckled with tiny purple flowers; the seed, slightly larger than a sunflower seed, is encased in a sturdy husk that adheres to the stalk until early winter. The window for harvesting is wide. The seed of *Scrophularia* is tiny, "smaller than a grain of mustard seed," and should the husk open and shatter, the gardener has lost the chance. Luckily, this autumn I am on time, and I seize the day, and the seeds, to ensure another generation.

Thirty-two years ago, seated on a 1952 Massey-Harris tractor, I seeded a cover crop of rye across this twenty-acre farm field, to bring it into production. Today, in the Herb Garden that nests between fields of squash and potatoes, I am harvesting a diversity of seeds, seeds that have served a diversity of cultures. The means of transport and tillage are simplified, and the silt loam soil is improved after decades of regenerative farming practice (based on traditional ecological methods). I've improved as a listener as well—the messages I receive from maple, larch, Queen Anne's lace, blackberry lily, balloon flowers still blooming, and the southwest winds are more nuanced, and lightly layered.

Among the rare beans I harvest, now that the dried pods crackle, is the cranberry-colored Shinnecock bean, a variety above all others that *belongs* here. Several years ago, at an organic farming conference in Syracuse, on the land of the Haudenosaunee, I visited the display table of a champion seed saver, Lisa Bloodnick, known for her generosity, and for maintaining a collection of one thousand bean varieties (including those mentioned at the start of this chapter). "I like the look of this one," I said. "What is the history?"

"That is the Shinnecock bean, and I was given it by a seed saver from Kentucky," Lisa said.

Surprised, engaged, I continued: "I am a neighbor of the Shinnecock Nation. My children attended school with Shinnecock children, and I gardened with a keeper of their seeds. Will you trust me with them?"

"They are yours!" said Lisa.

I returned to Long Island with a small packet and called Shane at his home on the reservation. His immediate question: "Are they cranberry colored?"

"Yes."

"I've heard about those beans, and I have been searching for years!" Shane replied, spirited.

The Shinnecock beans have been on a journey. Lisa was given them by a well-known third-generation seed saver, a Cherokee ethnobotanist from Wild Wood Farm in Artemus, Kentucky—Kris Hubbard. The story is this: Kris's grandfather was given beans by a fisherman from Long Island, and their name reports the provenance. Grown out for years at Wild Wood Farm, and by Lisa at Bloodnick Family Farm in the Susquehanna River Valley, and by yours truly, the cranberry beans, after an exodus of a hundred years, have now returned to their home ground. The variety in coloration reflects the years of travel, and the various gardens—the round beans vary from deep cranberry to a light rose to white artfully streaked with red, whether grown in Shinnecock soil or in Amagansett silt loam. When I shuck them, the story shimmers out.

Rare varieties of beans, a cranberry bean that journeyed forth (a century ago) from the Shinnecock Reservation and is now rematriated, an indigenous groundnut that twines where it will, Asian plants transplanted to North Atlantic island soil: a folly, some would say, and I might agree, but a folly that grafts onto the mission of a near neighbor (Marder's arboretum), one that is hopeful, inspiring, risky, exciting, playful, and unexpectedly effective. I recall a passage from Donald Culross Peattie: "The fabric is whole and strong; the web is intricate to unravel. We are ourselves part of it . . . These vital partnerships, these symbioses, are crossed threads in the web that goes back to plant life's beginnings."

Dawn, almost, though a waning crescent moon rises in the east, just preceding the sun, over the tangled hedge, over the tallest reach of the larch. The sky, an ocean of light, like a tide returning. To the south a thin river of mist caps the newly seeded field of rye. Here in the garden, within the net of moon-ocean-earth, every living thing reflects like a jewel. The auburn tips of timothy grass, the three-pointed leaves of *Liquidambar*, the red clusters of Sichuan peppers, the vines of *Apios americana* intertwined on young conifers. All that is flooded with dew flickers in the early light. There is something in the flight of the sparrow hawk, in her quick fall from the hedgerow to alight on silt loam, something familiar, remembered, just so, as daylight fills the furrows.

Chapter 10

GRAINS OF A GREAT WEB

O
Tree
into the world
Man
the chosen
Rose out of Chaos:
Song

—RONALD JOHNSON, *ARK*

By chance, today, lifting my wings from my study, I went out to greet wildness at Sagg Swamp, a hundred-acre preserve protected by the Nature Conservancy, not far from my home. A week ago, two feet of snow covered the ground, followed by a heavy rain and warming temperatures. Alone at the preserve, wading through wet loam, I acknowledged the accuracy of the place-name. Before I reached the boardwalk—a construction that hugs the reeds, rushes, and tangled vegetation and that leads the walker over swamp and wetlands (brilliant idea!)—I heard the slightly plaintive call of an unknown bird in a thicket of pepperidge and red maple. As I rounded the boardwalk trail and re-turned to the rich, damp earth, I heard a beat of wings, and then saw the feather tips of a sizable bird as it rose up from the swamp; with a graceful dancing descent, this great blue heron (*Ardea herodias*), with a wingspan of almost six feet, found a perch on a limb of red maple. A good choice for the heron, who now had a wide view of Solomon's Creek and the wetlands to the north. Within the wood, we were held in shadow, but the late light bathed the high branches of maple and tangled lichen clinging to bark, singing with gold. I stopped on the short wooden bridge over the weir to watch the bird—aware of me but unmoving—and to hear the gentle woodland echo of the creek flowing over the weir toward Sagg Pond. February, more winter to come, but the heron's cry, the aroma of silt, and the silver sound of Solomon's Creek whispered spring.

Sagg Swamp lies at the southern end of a series of vernal pools, kettle-hole ponds, streams, and marsh known as the Long Pond Greenbelt, a 3.5-mile ecological zone of roughly 1,000 acres created by the Wisconsin glacier 21,000 years ago, and reported to contain more rare species than any other site in New York State. A trail through the greenbelt follows the trace of an abandoned railway spur that once led from Bridgehampton village to Long Wharf, in Sag Harbor. Now the path has filled in with scrub oaks and low shrubs, while the wetter ground supports highbush blueberry, inkberry, sweet pepperbush, and staggerbush. Along the trail, on higher ground, are stands of pitch pine, white oak, red oak, hickory, and mountain laurel. The rarest plant species—white boneset, drowned horned rush, creeping St. John's wort, among many others—have adapted to survive on the edges of several ponds that expand and contract, depending on rainfall; from one year to the next, these resilient plants may be submerged or open to the air. Over a long period of years (and a carpet of leaves and limbs), through a process known as ecological succession, this zone of ponds will evolve to become a wooded swamp. Sagg Swamp can claim that title now, and as it drains to the south and toward the Atlantic, it empties into a body of water known as Sagg Pond.

I have spent many hours here, wading and walking, attentive to my children when they were young and to the shorebirds—and the place found expression in a poem, "Sagaponack":

> These reeds I see are full of tears:
>> summer rain simplified by grass,
>>> the pathway of water interrupted by matter.

> As it falls the blue heron steps
>> through grains of a great web.
>>> Sand, reeds, rain,

> translucent as years,
>> water tangible as tears
>>> on grasses by the salt pond.

> Called globes, each orb of rain
>> touched by grass, fluid in rest,
>>> reflects reeds, wings, the surface glitter of summer,
> clarity of dwelling in one body.

Peter Matthiessen, who lived in Sagaponack for fifty-five years, very near to the edge of the pond, was a well-known naturalist and a respected birder. In his classic book (one of thirty-three) *The Wind Birds* he describes the place, and I revel in his impeccable prose:

> From the west windows of my house, a fringe of trees parting the fields winds into view: here Sagg Pond, like a wide meadow river, curls down through miles of warm potato country to the sea. The Long Island farmland fills the landscape to the north and west and spreads toward the southward; Sagg Pond appears again, turned back upon itself by the hard white of the dunes, by the hard blue of the sea horizon. The pond bends like the shank of a great hook; it is now a mile across. But seasonally, in storm or flood, the pond is open to the sea. Then this lower reach is salt, a place of tidal creek and shallow flat which is today, as it has always been, a haunt of shorebirds.

In his handsome book *The Birds of Heaven: Travels with Cranes*, Matthiessen writes of an extremely rare visit by a young sandhill crane to the ocean beach that Sagg Pond borders. The bird, certainly blown way off course, remained for the winter on this Long Island beach, in the company of a great black-backed gull. I can imagine Matthiessen's engagement and attention on that morning in early spring when he heard the crane's call as the wandering bird passed over his writing shack, and over the reaching branches of the Siberian elm and the dawn redwood in the garden, in flight to places unknown.

Although herons are quite common among the marshes and along the shores of Sagg Pond, only three cranes have ever been spotted on Long Island. Cranes, the largest of all flying birds on earth, are the subject of legends by ancient peoples, and it is for good reason they are called the birds of heaven. The sandhill crane often flies at the height of a mile, and Eurasian cranes ascend to three miles above sea level to cross the Himalayas. Considered an auspicious species by the Greeks, the bird appears in *The Iliad:* "The Trojans went forth with a cry and shout, like cranes, / like the cry of cranes when they fly toward heaven." In Greek legend, Palamedes invented the alphabet based on the flight patterns of migrating cranes. The Chinese believed these great birds, *xian-he*, transported messages on their backs from one sky world to another. In a lyrical passage in his novel *The Echo Maker*, Richard Powers tells how the Aztecs referred to themselves as the Crane People, and one Anishinabe clan was named after the great birds—Ajijak or Businassee: the echo makers.

The lineage of present-day cranes extends back to the Eocene, almost sixty million years ago. The birds of heaven, some standing five feet tall with a wingspan of eight feet, migrate across continents, and to our species they are symbolic of longevity, good fortune, harmony, and fidelity. When we listen to the crane's call, according to Aldo Leopold, "we hear the trumpet in the orchestra of evolution . . . Their annual return is the clicking of the geologic clock."

For Matthiessen they are also a symbol of what we stand to lose unless we reverse our assault on wild habitats and somehow learn to work in harmony with the natural order. Cranes are considered an umbrella species—in order to ensure the survival of these birds that travel such great distances, it is essential to conserve diverse ecosystems, an incentive to protect broad expanses of land and water and diverse forms of life. In a plea for sanity to his fellow *sapiens*, also blown way off course, Matthiessen writes: "One way to grasp the main perspectives of environment and biodiversity is to understand the origins and precious nature of a single living form, a single manifestation of the miracle of existence; if one has truly understood a crane—or a leaf or a cloud or a frog—one has understood everything."

Matthiessen's travels, often on research expeditions, to New Guinea, Nepal, Australia, Alaska, the rain forests of Peru, the Amazon, in a way defined him. But for five decades he returned to his home and writing studio in Sagaponack, a brief curlew's flight from the Atlantic, (and a short distance on Sagg Road from my home). It was here, in a horse stable reborn as a Zendo, as a student and later as Muryo Roshi, that he practiced Zen (*roshi* signifies a teacher; literally it translates as "a venerable old one"). I too sat in meditation here, grateful for Muryo's teaching—and as friend and apprentice to master woodworker and monk Hans Hokanson, I built the door into the Zendo (the gateless gate), the simple ceremonial table, and the bench at the entrance. So close to the Atlantic! When the waves were strong, the ocean would sift through the silence, as would the sound of Canadian geese in flight, or the crack of oak in the woodstove, and my meditation sometimes found expression in a poem, such as "Winter":

Raw radiance: a thousand birds
on the straw field of frost,
and winter's salt light on the mat.

The rip and pearl of paper—
mind's rasp, geese steer into sleep.
Will my breath return to speech,
or stay to posture with the absolute?

Two words surface often during the practice of Zen:
"Pay attention!" and throughout the course of writing this
book, in a time unsettled, chaotic, *on fire*, under the spell of
a global pandemic, I have heard the echo of those words.
And following my immersion in tree literature, I have
been influenced daily by the name given to a rare tree
species, a survivor of the prehistoric world, unchanged in
millions of years, "discovered" in Australia in 1994. The
Wollemi pine derives its name from the Aboriginal word
wollumnii, meaning "look around you."

At the northern end of the Long Pond Greenbelt, our
house is circled by red oaks and white oaks, a few
hickory trees, various conifers we have planted, and four
impressive pitch pines (*Pinus rigida*, locally called black
pine) that soar to sixty feet above the sandy soil. Though
the glaciers departed here eleven thousand years ago,
I am keenly aware of their passage—our dwelling

rests on the rim of kettle holes to the east and to the south, now wooded, each three hundred feet across. As the Laurentide Ice Sheet withdrew, great blocks of ice pressed and melted into the earth—the cavern that remains is aptly called a kettle. The understory of this rolling landscape comes to life in May, when the abundant mountain laurel (*Kalmia latifolia*), a bushy, rhododendron-like shrub, bursts into clusters of white-and-pink flowers that spread like stars over each bush. I am thankful to Enrique Salmón's beautiful book *Iwígara: The Kinship of Plants and People* for the knowledge that mountain laurel has another name: spoonwood (a profuse plant favored by Indigenous people, for the making of implements and utensils). Last spring, I waded into the center of a sprawling stand of laurel and found a thick, shapely branch (I counted fifty rings in the wood), no longer alive, but perfectly seasoned for carving. The wood is handsome, extremely hard, honey colored, with a fluid grain: qualities that provide a starting block for a graceful spoon.

After a very wet spring and summer, this year our yard and surrounding woods were inundated with an astonishing array of mushrooms, the fruiting bodies of underground fungal life. So I welcomed the arrival of *Entangled Life*, a book penned by a young forest detective, a celebration of the life fruiting in my wooded yard. The author—whose name is perfectly attuned to his subject and his passion—Merlin Sheldrake, begins his book, subtitled *How Fungi Make Our Worlds, Change Our Minds, and Shape Our Futures*, with these three words: "Fungi are everywhere." Yes, I thought, I see the fruit. But of course, what we don't see is much more expansive, and of greater significance for a biotic community. The most famous example is located in Oregon, a honey fungus at least two thousand years old and weighing hundreds of tons. *Armillaria solidipes*, considered to be one of the largest organisms on earth, covers an area of about four square miles, and it is possible that even larger *Armillaria* live underground in places yet to be discovered. Aboveground, the aspen grove in Utah's Fishlake National Forest, eighty thousand years old and weighing in at thirteen million pounds, rivals *Armillaria* for sheer bulk. Can a fungal network or an aspen grove be counted as an individual, a single organism? This is an open question, and it leads to some creative discussion.

Sheldrake reports that somewhere between 2.2 and 3.8 million species of fungi populate the earth, perhaps 10 times the number of plant species, though at present only 6 percent have been described. Fungi have existed for over a billion years, and when the first plants ventured out of the water, fungi provided root systems—for tens of millions of years—until plants evolved their own. Biologists and ecologists are only just beginning to uncover the mystery of this ancient collaboration between fungi and plants, and to recognize the beauty, the value, and the complexity of such reciprocal relationships. Here we are at the heart—or circulatory system—of an underground social network.

Dr. Samuel Johnson, in his famous dictionary—published in 1755, a brilliant achievement, idiosyncratic and influential, accomplished in only eight years and listing forty thousand words—defined the word *network* with this puzzling sentence: "Any thing reticulated or decussated, at equal distances, with interstices between the intersections." Hmm, I don't find that very helpful, though I do have a clear picture when Suzanne Simard describes, in her book *Finding the Mother Tree*, the more than one hundred species of mycorrhizal fungi that live in the forest of paper birch and Douglas fir she studies. She writes of this teeming network as "an intricately woven rug," and she quotes Subiyay (Bruce Miller) of the Skokomish Nation: "There is an intricate and vast system of root and fungi that keeps the forest strong." Forest ecologist Simard continues, acknowledging the Indigenous wisdom she has learned from: "I have come full circle to stumble onto some of the indigenous ideals: Diversity matters. And everything in the universe is connected—between the forests and prairies, the land and the water, the sky and the soil, the spirits and the living, the people and all other creatures."

The relationship between mycorrhizal fungi and plants has existed for about 450 million years—90 percent of plants today depend upon this relationship. Astonishingly, mycorrhizal fungi compose one-third to one-half of the living mass of soils. Sheldrake calls this "the ultimate mutualism," mutualism being a type of symbiosis that benefits two or more organisms, often a stable interconnection that can last for a very long time. "Symbiosis is a ubiquitous feature of life," says Sheldrake, and tracing the relationships between fungi and plants leads him to take measure of our human identities. Just as the existence of fungi suggests that we question our presumed categories, so too does the existence of a hidden half of nature, the unseen, lead to similar questions. It is common to speak of an eco-system that surrounds us, outside of us, but Sheldrake believes that we are ecosystems too, "a complex tangle of relationships only now becoming known." The phi-losopher Daniel Dennett, toward the end of his book *Darwin's Dangerous Idea*, poses an inevitable question: "Am I an organism, or a community, or both?" The Swedish biologist Svante Pääbo believes that our hu-man genome is a mosaic.

So how do you classify a mosaic life-form? Microbiologist W. Ford Doolittle, in an article that refers to a universal tree, suggests that "the impulse to classify or-ganisms is ancient . . . as is the desire to have classification reflect the 'natural order.'" Charles Darwin, contemplating that natural order, famously made a sketch of a tree in his 1837 notebook (labeled *B*), and he wrote two words above it: "I think." I possess a handsome facsimile of the first edi-tion of the *On the Origin of Species* (published in 1859), and included on a thin foldout sheet of paper is a delicate dia-gram intended to exhibit the principles of natural selection. The diagram is drawn in the graceful shape of two trees, and Darwin is confident that the image "will aid us in un-derstanding this rather perplexing subject." A hundred and sixty-three years later, the subject is still perplexing, though the branches and buds of that original tree have been trans-mogrified. When David Quammen was doing research for his book *The Tangled Tree*, he was told by W. Ford Doolittle: "Whether or not there is a tree of life . . . depends a whole lot on what we mean by a tree of life."

What we mean varies, of course, depending on whom

you ask. Merlin Sheldrake points out that the metaphor has been a subject of debate for decades. Darwin himself wondered if the "coral of life" might work better, but he returned to wood. The geneticist Richard Lewontin suggested a playful alternative: "an elaborate bit of macramé." With his ears open and his eyes on the underground, Sheldrake has heard a number of variant metaphors to describe life: a network, a rhizome, a cobweb, among others. Given the folly of searching for the one word, one metaphor to represent so grand a thing as life itself—in evolution for nearly four billion years—perhaps we should consult a poet. Emily Dickinson, in her poem beginning "I had not minded—Walls" writes:

> But 'tis a single Hair—
> A filament—a law
> A Cobweb—wove in Adamant—

I may digress, I know, but only to better understand the "intricately woven rug," and I write in a time when we are all wise to ask questions. The Greek root for *adamant* is kin to our English word *invincible.* Circa 345 BCE, Theophrastus, the favorite student of Aristotle, called the father of plant ecology and author of *Enquiry into Plants,* used the word *adamant* to describe the hardest crystalline gem then known, the emery stone of Naxos. The old friendship of stone and man I discussed in an earlier chapter is woven into the evolution of species on earth.

In her own way, Dickinson too was searching for a natural law, as was Darwin, as will the poets and naturalists of coming generations, in order to gain wisdom

and direction from it, we must hope. Merlin Sheldrake
nominates "a new poster organism for evolution," and—
surprise!—the form of life that rises to mind is fungal
mycelium. As it happens, the fine branching structures
within plant cells are called arbuscules—little trees—and
this is where plant and fungus exchange. "A filament—a
law," though as we are learning still, one that is intricate,
interconnected, and branching out in many directions.

The oaks, hickories, mountain laurel, and occasional
glacial erratic rock that surround my home are covered
with lichen in arrays of siskin green and primrose yellow, as if an abstract artist slapped thick paint on gray
bark and stone to introduce some color (my color guide
is *Werner's Nomenclature of Colours,* by Patrick Syme and
Abraham Gottlob Werner, published in Edinburgh in
1821, the book used by Darwin to describe colors in nature on his HMS *Beagle* voyage). The texture of lichen
tends to curl. The origin of lichen, called the gateway
organism for symbiosis, is a mystery, though the earliest
fossil evidence dates from about four hundred million
years ago. One in five fungal species are known to form
into lichens—to lichenize—should there be an alga
species accepting of the compact. If you have heard
the jingle once, you will have a memory of it: "A fungus took a likin' to an alga." When the Swiss botanist
Simon Schwendener suggested, in 1869, that a lichen

was not a single organism, his theory was loudly re-
jected (including by Beatrix Potter!). However, within
the next few decades, as more and more evidence of
symbiotic relationships was discovered, Schwendener's
theory became an accepted biological principle.

A relationship is forged when the fungus provides
protection and acquires nutrients both for itself and for
the algal partner; the alga in turn captures light and
carbon dioxide to make sugars and provide energy.
The resulting organism—a lichen—has "changed
the face of the planet," according to Sheldrake. In
the new organism, each partner achieves what it was
unable to do alone. Individual identity is given over
to what Sheldrake names with a beautiful phrase: "a
metabolic 'song.'" Lichens now cover the surface of
about 8 percent of the earth, and their acquired skill
is to break down and dissolve rock (a process known
as weathering). Following a glacier retreat, lichens are
the first organisms to appear, and when they perish
and decompose, they provide the first soils as a basis
for a germinating ecosystem. Strangely, given the success of lichens as a foundational life-form, because of
their symbiotic nature, they resist categorization, and
they are often named after the fungal half of their composition. Trevor Goward, who has added thirty thousand lichen specimens to the collection he curates at
the University of British Columbia, observes that this
gateway organism by its very composition teaches us
things about living interactions.

The visionary biologist Lynn Margulis thought so
too when she proposed that the first eukaryotic cells

(introduced in chapter 1) were very similar to lichens. She admired this ancient mutualistic organism that embodies innovation and partnership. When Margulis first discussed the theory of endosymbiosis in 1967, her ideas were dismissed in the same fashion as those of Schwendener a century before. Eventually, over the following decades, with others building on Margulis's work and with the assistance of new genetic tools, this theory revised the history of life as we know it. At certain critical points in the history of evolution, separate single-celled organisms (prokaryotes) merged into one (the birth of eukaryotes, cells with nuclei), and all complex life arose from this "reciprocal alchemy" (Suzanne Simard's phrase). The essence of the theory is contained in a sentence by Merlin Sheldrake: "Within eukaryotic cells, distant branches of the tree of life entwine and melt into an inseparable new lineage; they fuse . . . as fungal hyphae do." And we are part of the tangle, or, if you prefer, the "metabolic song." Daniel Dennett called it "one of the most beautiful ideas I've ever encountered." Dennett's observation is really a celebration of life—the meaning of the Greek prefix *eu-* is "good." Endosymbiosis led to the creation of eukaryotes, and such are we.

Under the oaks and hickories in my wooded yard in this wet year, a most unusual plant flourished in its own way, a ghost plant that relies on the nourishment of the unseen mycorrhizal network. I am familiar with the plant as Indian pipe, though at first sight I assumed it was a fungus. So many Indian pipes pushed through the carpet of leaves this year that I kneeled in close for a beetle's-eye view. The slim stalks, rising only six to ten inches above the leaf litter, are pure white, almost translucent. A sort of bell drops from the top of each stalk, and only when you zoom in can you identify the shape of a flower. If you linger for a time, you will see a bumblebee on a visit to this odd, endearing plant, as it stumbles from bell to bell, clinging to white petals, pollinating, intent on nectar. In this comic yet graceful dance, the bee dwarfs the flower, and gathers pollen from an upside-down peace-pipe plant devoid of chlorophyll.

Monotropa uniflora, also known as ice plant, bird's nest, or ghost plant, is a member of the Ericaceae, or heath, family, a relative of blueberry and mountain laurel, both of which flourish in this woodland. However, not a single cousin or neighbor even remotely resembles the Indian pipe. *Monotropa* (in Greek: "one turn") is a plant labeled as a mycoheterotroph; it does not photosynthesize—a character trait shared by only 1 percent of the plant world—and must therefore gather energy from another source. That source is the network of mycorrhizal fungi that also feeds the oaks and hickories— so trees, fungi, and ghost plant are all interconnected within the wood web. Mycoheterotrophs are unique because they are takers, or, the term I prefer, full-time receivers—testament "to the fact that shared mycorrhizal networks can support a unique way of life," in Sheldrake's words.

Throughout late summer and into the autumn, this rare plant thrusts through a forest of leaves, here and there, never as a single stem, but rising like a grove of little white trees, some stems or flowers streaked with carmine or peach-blossom red, waiting to receive a passing bumblebee. In an impressive gesture, following pollination each stem stands up, and soon the ripened seeds within the bell are released into the wind. Wherever and whenever it first formed, *Monotropa* found a way to produce a flower in unusual fashion, without the aid of the sun—an eccentric angiosperm, you might say. No wonder that Charles Darwin called the rise of the angiosperms, 140 million years ago, "an abominable mystery." Having witnessed the dexterity of the bumblebee on the bell of the ghost plant, and aware of the mycorrhizal web branching and provisioning beneath, I will amend his expression: a mystery woven through the filament and grains of a great web.

Chapter 11

THE MOUNTING SAP

You walk a stranger in a vegetating world; then with
an inward click the shutter of some profounder level
of consciousness uncloses and admits you to sentience
of the mounting sap.

—MARY AUSTIN, *THE LAND OF JOURNEYS' ENDING*

The valley spirit never dies;
It is the woman, primal mother.

—LAO TSU, *TAO TE CHING*

They return to their sett each night, and spend the day in darkness, within the soil. They are surrounded, embraced by the mineral dark, the mycelium network, the underground we do not see, and they find home within it. Home enough for generations to endure for two hundred years or more, if they are not disturbed. Though we shared space on a hillside in Cornwall for a decade, just above the granite rock that solidifies the coast, I saw a badger only once, slowed for several seconds in the glare of my headlights as I descended Raginnis Hill through the narrow lane. Not once, in years of clearing ground in the cliff meadows, planting spuds, hoeing rows of garlic, harvesting tobacco leaves, not once did I encounter a badger, though, as frequent visitors to the damp of the nighttime meadows, they helped themselves to what I planted—carrots, radishes, and turnips, a feast for those who are designed to dig. As luck would have it, my children were beside me in the car that evening on Raginnis Hill, and of course we had an immediate frame of reference.

When we meet Badger within the first pages of *The Wind in the Willows*, Ratty replies to Mole's question about the inhabitants of the Wild Wood: "And then there's Badger, of course. He lives right in the heart of it; wouldn't live anywhere else, either, if you paid him to do it. Dear old Badger! Nobody interferes with him. They'd better not."

Badgers are short and stocky, connected with the earth, formidable, and they keep to themselves. I never interfered, though I often stood in wonder on the soft ground—peppered like a moonscape—above the sett, in the field at the lane's end, the place the badgers had chosen to dig in and to claim as residence. As I built my own home just down the lane, I knew there was something to learn from these shy animals with a powerful instinct toward dwelling. At a very young age, as he watched me erecting walls and rafters, my first son, Levin, was aware of the choice made by this other species. His classic statement about our mustelid neighbors is embedded in a poem I wrote for my son: "Misser bagger lives down olles!"

The poet T'ao Ch'ien (365–427), one of the initiators of the Chinese rivers-and-mountains tradition, writes of returning to the hills and mountains he loves, to nurture "simplicity among these fields and gardens, / home again." A word he employs, *tzu-yàn*, has archetypal

significance for the Chinese rivers-and-mountains tradition, and this word has influenced me throughout the
writing of this book, though the meaning is not easy to
grasp. David Hinton, author and translator of ancient
Chinese, comments that the term is often simplified in
translation, read as a synonym for *nature*, but nature, like
the tao, is the source of ten thousand things, the gate to
all mystery, impossible to summarize, or even to name.
Wilderness in ancient Chinese thought is a "dynamic
cosmology," broader and deeper than one word—such
as *nature*—can contain, and we are participants in it. In
rivers-and-mountains poetry—a literary tradition spanning two millennia—this cosmology inspires a sense of
belonging, of coming home. *Tzu-yan* literally means "self-
ablaze," which leads to "self-so," and then "spontaneous"
or "natural." Hinton, however, opens the gate of meaning to offer another translation: "occurrence appearing of
itself." To follow the thought, imagine the ten thousand
things of the tao coming forth spontaneously from the
generative source. Not easy to grasp, but I come near to
it when I walk through a grove of oak and hickory and
hear the percussive beat of wings as a flicker rides the air
from branch to branch. Or when, within another wood,
I hear the music of a gentle waterfall rise from stone, as
melodic as an étude by Chopin, the clear water reflective
of spruce needles and bark, the blue sky as a cap over the
conifer canopy.

In the prologue, I summoned Bashō: "Each day is a
journey and the journey itself home." Peter Matthiessen,
author, naturalist, Zen roshi, friend, influenced by a passage in Carl Jung, writes eloquently in *The Snow Leopard*

of his own singular journey, and of a universal one: "The search may begin with a restless feeling, as if we were being watched. One turns in all directions and sees nothing. Yet one senses that there is a source for this deep restlessness; and the path that leads there is not a path to a strange place, but the path home."

The word *tzu-yan* envisions earth "as a boundless generative organism," in Hinton's words, an enveloping present. Within the sister term *yu-chou*—translated as "time and space"—*yu* refers to "space itself as living habitation," and the Chinese character for *chou* depicts a seed within a dwelling, beneath a roof (the sky, or heaven). Here is a primal cosmology within which we participate, moment by moment—the path home is the space we inhabit.

"The seeds are coming home to us," she says, and she is a vessel for the stories held within seeds, a Mohawk woman who descends from a long line of women who cared for soil and plants with reverence and skill. In generation after generation, it was the women who nurtured food crops and served as seed keepers, who held in their hands the harvest that would ensure another harvest. The ancestor of this sacred inheritance is the first woman who stepped onto the earth carrying seeds, to sing the world awake. Rowen White refers to the creation story, and of her role as daughter and mother, member of the Mohawk community of Akwesasne, descended from women who were "creative, fertile, fierce, loving, complex, insightful, wise, resourceful, and ever-changing." Seeds absent from Native lands, sometimes for centuries, are now, through some inspired and creative alliances, being returned to their communities of origin. There is a beautiful word to describe this cultural and evolutionary process—*rematriation*—a word I first heard spoken by Rowen in a room filled with attentive growers and seed stewards, those whose livelihoods depend on the quality of their caring for soil.

Rematriation: the word is full of earthen color and texture when it is voiced by Rowen, who embodies the sound and sense of it, as she does when she speaks of seeds: "The seeds, my teachers, were growing me." The word is resonant and multilayered, and, like living seeds, it carries human stories within it. Stories passed on by generations of those who viewed seeds as relatives, not as part of an inventory but as living populations. Rematriation is intergenerational, a cultural reconciliation among Indigenous peoples tracing the original agreement between plants and humans and in dialogue with such critical issues as food sovereignty, seed sovereignty, and social justice. Enrique Salmón writes that "the responsibility of growing food for one's community is connected to one's identity as a member of the community . . . This sense of being-ness is tied to the history of the people on a landscape."

For centuries the Indigenous people of our continent were removed from their ancestral lands, their homelands, systematically, by force or trickery or broken treaty, beginning in the sixteenth century. We know this; our American culture is stained by the process, but still our culture continues to ignore the depth of the wound. For Indigenous people, land is at the foundation of all things, not as property, but as the source of "food, water, medicine, and all nutritional needs for every living organism . . . Because of the land, it is possible to live"—in the words of Simon Ortiz, an Acoma Pueblo writer and scholar. Alfonso Ortiz, who was a member of the Pueblo of Ohkay Owingeh and for over twenty years a professor of anthropology at the University of New Mexico, wrote this in an essay titled "Origins: Through Tewa Eyes":

> That the Tewa see all life as beginning within the earth, like the corn plant that has sustained us for centuries, is manifest in our sacred places: The kiva, the ceremonial center, which represents the primordial home under the lake; the "earth mother earth navel middle place" in every village; and our mountaintop shrines—"earth navels"— shaped of stones and boulders.

Rowen was born in a swirling blizzard in the Akwesasne land that nestles along the Saint Lawrence River; her Mohawk given name is Kanienten:hawi, "she brings the snow." At age seventeen she remembers experiencing a kind of awakening, more a sense of coming home, when she found herself working with plants on a farm in western Massachusetts. Since that time, she has lived in service to seeds, celebrating seeds, honoring seeds "as a prayer embodied. They are witness to the past," she says, "tiny time capsules of life's rich and layered stories." Now living in Nevada City, California, she founded Sierra Seeds, with a desire to inspire reverence and action:

> Sierra Seeds seeks to reseed imaginations of a more beautiful and nourishing world through uplifting and mentoring emerging mentors, changemakers, visionaries, creative humans who are making nourishing contributions at the intersections of the landscape of food and seed sovereignty and cultural revitalization, who are cultivating foodways that grow from a foundation of belonging, connection, and culture.

To do so, she advises that we need a new lexicon to discuss seed matters, plant cultivation, food production. I fully agree. The words we choose prescribe our attitudes—no, our beings and aspirations—and can also inspire change. In addition to the lost words—referenced in chapter 7—words that have served to connect us with other species and the land we inhabit, there are concepts, ideograms perhaps, that serve to integrate rather than to alienate. Rowen is careful to choose words that cultivate a culture of belonging, and she voices the word *rehydrate* as a way to revive ancestral memory. And this is precisely what seeds embody—in caring hands, once watered, a bloom of ancestral memory rises to the surface. Seeds are living things and carry *the spirit of the land* within a protective seed coat. Cultural foodways (or relational foodways), rather than the more common term *food systems*, add some vibrancy to a living network that is at the source of our well-being. In an eloquent discussion of language, community wholeness, and sustainability, Simon Ortiz writes: "*Haatse* [land] . . . is the instigator of language; in fact, language initiates and originates in the relationship we, as a human community, have with the land."

Through centuries of colonization and displacement, seeds have been dispersed and separated from their communities of origin—the people who planted and preserved them, and were nourished by them—with many varieties lost along the way. Some have found home in public or private collections, such as land grant universities (the University of Michigan being one), the USDA Center for Agricultural Resources Research in Fort Collins, Colorado (a national seed bank), or the Seed Savers Exchange in Iowa. (To be fair, seeds specialize in dispersal, but not by artificial means.) To return seeds to the original caretakers is a process that involves negotiation, establishing trust, and also spiritual and emotional focus and work. The Indigenous Seed Keepers Network (ISKN), a program of the Native American Food Sovereignty Alliance (NAFSA), is a "shade tree of support" to the work of regional and tribal seed initiatives, promoting diversity for future generations through the growing, collecting, and sharing of heirloom seeds and plants. NAFSA was formed to unite communities and organizations, along with tribal governments, to enliven native foodways; originally, members of thirteen tribes gathered to share knowledge and experience of agricultural practices, seed saving, and native foods. ISKN provides mentorship, training, and advocacy support relating to seed policy, as a field map to encourage ethical seed stewardship, and as a guideline for Indigenous communities to protect their seeds from biopiracy and the absurdity of seed patenting.

Repatriation is listed in my edition of the *Oxford English Dictionary* (*OED*): "to restore a person to his own country" (a definition likely to be updated in a following edition). *Rematriation* does not appear, though that too will be corrected in a future edition, we hope, and what truly matters is that cultural reconciliation continues. ISKN defines the word thus: "It simply means back to Mother Earth, a return to our origins, to life and co-creation, honoring the life-giving force of the Divine Feminine." The words have resonance, deserve to be remembered, and are instructive for a culture that must soon agree on a way to reinhabit our planet.

With my wife, Megan, on a kind of pilgrimage to the land where she was born, I visited Grandmother Flordemayo on the high plains of New Mexico, fifty miles east of Albuquerque, at sixty-one hundred feet, in Estancia, "the place of rest." Flordemayo is a *curandera espiritu*, a healer of divine spirit, born in the highlands of Central America, and now a member of the International Council of Thirteen Indigenous Grandmothers. We met at her home in the heart of the village and followed her (on a spirited ride) out to the Path, a healing center on forty acres of land exposed to sun and wind and a great sky. Standing there in such openness—so small is one being!—I was strangely nourished by the infinity of space.

In the center of the Path is the gathering place, the Hogan, and the Seed Temple, where corn, beans, squash,

grains, and herbs are stored in a controlled environment—"each one a whole universe of sustenance," in
Rowen's words. When we entered the cool earthen cellar, lined with shelves holding glass jars filled with living
memory, I imagined the badgers—in a vastly different climate—underground, at home, secure within the earth.
The mission here is to conserve and distribute open-pol-
linated and heirloom varieties, and to cultivate the culture of belonging that Rowen speaks of; the Path col-
laborates with other seed growers of the Southwest and
with sister organizations such as the Rocky Mountain
Seed Alliance.

Grandmother Flordemayo has said that seeds have
a spirit, but they lack a voice. Rowen White imagines
a voice: "We are still here. We are still vibrant. We are
interconnected. We help nourish each other."

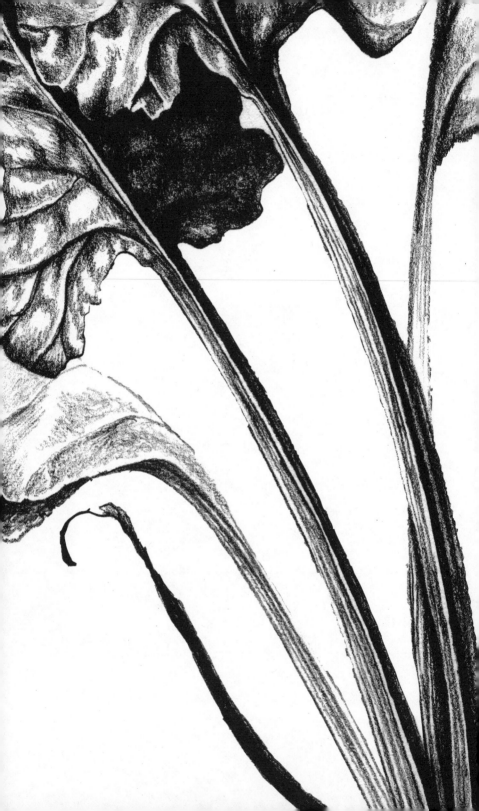

Chapter 12

FILTERS OF THE EARTH

But now all was changed, even the air. Instead of the rough and arid gusts that I had met with before, there was a soft and scented breeze. A sound like water drifted down from the heights: it was the wind in the forests.

—JEAN GIONO, *THE MAN WHO PLANTED TREES*

For the world is a nest, and an immense power holds the inhabitants of the world in this nest.

—GASTON BACHELARD, *THE POETICS OF SPACE*

Our wooden house on the Penwith Peninsula nested on a very steep hillside, with stairs leading up to the front door and an entrance below at ground level leading into the cellar, facing east as the hillside descends to granite, sea-foam, and the expanse of Mount's Bay and the Lizard Peninsula in the distance. We lived above, and on one particular spring, lured by the 6' × 3' opening (before I installed a cellar door), a wren moved in below. I remember this bright bird, not only because of her grand, melodious song, but because her choice of residence encouraged a poem to fledge. This spring, forty years later, I watched a Carolina wren wing in and out—beak full of oak leaves, bark, and string—building, nesting on a high shelf

within our front porch, here, on another peninsula, the
far reach of Long Island. The poem, titled "The Wren,"
returns with the bird:

My good-luck charm—
    the white, wailing, teeth-bared bone hyena
        wears on his back

the purple petals of May
    from the West Country hedge
        as he stands in a drift of picked flowers

on teak, between seeds, songs, and *Hope Abandoned.*

Like the wren
    in the perfect circle of her house
        under my house—

I ask the companions
    lightness and burden
        to nest inside: wings and music.

Here—inseparable by conduct from poetry—
    the work of the eyes, and of the heart—
        I am infinitely in the open!

The blackthorn hedge floods with Spring weight—
    and in my room the things I am blinded by
        release to melody: sky!

I always hesitate to explain the shape or form a poem makes (impossible!), but in this case the reader should know I had not abandoned hope, quite to the contrary. The reference is to the luminous book by Nadezhda Mandelstam, writer and wife of the Russian poet Osip Mandelstam, who suffered and perished under Stalin's regime. In the Russian language, *nadezhda* means "hope." The poem invokes Orpheus, universal poet and singer, as a vessel, one who receives.

Birds like our present house: the inside of it. In the words of the Nobel Prize–winning Polish poet Czeslaw Milosz: "For our house is open, there are no keys in the doors." Cardinal, chickadee, downy woodpecker, finch, chipping sparrow, nuthatch, all visit throughout the year—primarily to alight on the feeders that hang near our kitchen window, a short glide from several pines and cedars and a tangled wisteria vine. As the weather warms, and our sliding glass doors are often open, the inside of our saltbox looks, well, quite similar to the outside. When our children were young, they questioned: "Our house is surrounded by trees. Why do we have a forest inside too?"

The ceiling of our main room is sixteen feet tall, full of light provided by two skylights, and multiple avocado trees (we planted several pits) long ago reached the apex. Two ficus trees (one has traveled with us since 1980) branch out to claim the western region of the room. Assorted other plants—ranging from a robust jade to several aloes (perpetually multiplying) and *Clivia miniata*—provide a thick understory. Bright, warm, decorated with leaves and branches: an environment inviting to avian species.

On a mild day, as my wife, Megan, and I enjoyed the fresh air of early May, seated on the deck, a tufted titmouse, curious and perky, danced by us and into the house. We entered by a different door to gently recommend the outside woodland to our guest. Now she was joined, inside, by her mate, and two couples—the titmouse pair and us—improvised a dance until the winged ones finally found the open door.

The following morning, seated beside the sliding glass door of my study, engrossed in my reading (*The Tangled Tree: A Radical New History of Life*), I sensed a quick movement outside on the cedar steps, where Bella, by habit, basks in the southern exposure. Brindled, full of fur, a gifted bird dog, she seemed strangely unconcerned by the theatrics of a bouncing 5.5-inch-tall tufted titmouse. The same bird, returning. She hopped from one step to the other, flew up to the handrail, now down to Bella's step, closing in. Bella glanced in the direction of her visitor, though her lack of interest could be summed up in the popular expression: "Really?"

The bird was focused on Bella's tail, the extremity the greatest distance from teeth, and, for a diminutive nest builder, a forest of fur. Now only inches away from the dog's tail, something caught the eye of the architect. A prize, there for the taking, one step down, less risky than the tail—a sizable tangle of canine fluff. Redirected, she dove, and with a nimble move secured the fur in her beak and returned to the handrail. She pinned the prize to the cedar with her tiny feet and, using her beak, stretched and shaped the tangle for a reason known only to a tufted titmouse. (Perhaps while witness to a similar ritual the first human weavers of wool learned the art of carding). The French writer Jules Michelet observed that a bird is a worker without tools: "A bird's tool is its own body." Her beak now stuffed with Bella's brindled hair, and with an impulse to nest, the agile mother flew off, to build.

I encountered the words of Michelet in a beautiful book by the French philosopher Gaston Bachelard, *The Poetics of Space*, and I remembered his chapter, read many years ago, simply entitled "Nests." Bachelard, who writes in this book of house and universe, drawers and chests, shells, corners, and "the phenomenology of roundness," speaks of both nest and home as weaving a "sturdy web of intimacy." On day number three, after Megan had brushed Bella and left an offering on those same steps, the nest builder returned again to gather. With her beak full, still calling to her mate, she paused her purposeful flight for some seconds to light very close to Megan. *Reciprocity* is a lovely word, and though we lose the meaning in description, sometimes it is in the air—even shared by diverse species—as it was in this gesture, and in the risky dance on the steps, the song of the titmouse.

I found the phenomenologist philosopher again this spring, within my study, instructive in his chapter on nests. He imagines the things of this world as primal images, and he quotes the Russian poet Boris Pasternak: "For it is obvious that the image *alone* can keep pace with nature." Bachelard examines nests, close up, and is proud to name the architect that I too have admired: "I become once more a man of the fields and thickets, and a bit vain at being able to hand on my knowledge to a child, I say: 'This is the nest of a titmouse.'" I can easily imagine that nest, Gaston, it is very close by, and I know the builder. The philosopher continues: "A nest . . . is a precarious thing, and yet it sets us to *daydreaming of security* . . . And so, when we examine a nest, we place ourselves at the origin of confidence in the world . . . The nest is a lyrical bouquet of leaves."

The trees arrived today, three boxes shipped from Copemish, Michigan, each box a nest for eleven trees, and on each container pot a label: "*Sequoia sempervirens*, Hardy East Coast Redwoods." When we opened each box, what a wonder! Slender redwood saplings, three and a half feet in length, nestled together, each main spine taped to a bamboo stake, short needlelike leaves a shining green, even after the significant journey. Perhaps because this project is quite unique, these baby redwoods seem to embody the charisma of their California relatives. They are ready to be planted, and we've prepared the site in Bridgehampton, on the campus of the Hayground School. The children too are ready to plant, and several young students have met the mother trees.

Megan and I received a call from David Milarch, founder of Archangel Ancient Tree

Archive (AATA), in late winter—we had met a couple of times in the past—and he voiced a request. "I'm sitting here in my greenhouse in Copemish surrounded by about a hundred hardy Long Island redwood clones, and we would really like to send them home." Copemish is the home base for AATA, and the place where cuttings of champion trees are cloned through an intricate horticultural process, monitored, nurtured, and grown to sapling stage in greenhouses.

Our reply was immediate: "And we would like to welcome them!"

Several years ago, on a trip to the East End of Long Island, Milarch had been introduced to seven coastal redwoods, well established at an innovative garden tucked in the oak woods of East Hampton—LongHouse Reserve: sixteen acres of ornamental diversity and art founded by textile designer Jack Lenor Larsen. *Sequoia sempervirens* thriving on the East Coast? The natural habitat for these iconic trees is a thin stretch of land 30 miles wide and 450 miles long, extending from central California to the Oregon border. Redwoods are the lone survivors of the forests that covered the earth during the Cretaceous period, 144 to 166 million years ago. They are not known to favor frost, though at LongHouse Reserve they have weathered twenty-five winters. Considered mild for the northeast region, winter temperatures, even here in USDA Zone 7, can occasionally plunge to single digits. It was David Milarch who labeled these trees "hardy East Coast redwoods."

There is some mystery concerning the arrival of the redwoods to LongHouse, and now that we are stewards

of the offspring of these trees, I am curious of the provenance. Larsen, the magician responsible for the diverse
and colorful palette of the sixteen-acre garden, passed
away in 2020, and the horticulturist at Rockefeller Center
who bequeathed the trees passed on several years ago (we
will continue our search). But here they are, champions
in their own way, and with a natural connection with
the mission of AATA. Once again the Marders, a family
of arborists, and collaborators with Milarch, enter the
story—Mica Marder climbed the redwoods and took the
cuttings that were transferred to Michigan to be grown
out—in a controlled horticultural procedure—and now
returned as cloned saplings to Hayground.

AATA began as Champion Trees over twenty-five
years ago, with a seminal idea to save the genetics of the
strongest trees of multiple species, and to plant arbors of
the cloned offspring in well-chosen landscapes. The mission of AATA: to *propagate* the world's most important
old growth trees, to *archive* the genetics of ancient trees
in living libraries, and to *reforest* the earth with offspring
of champion trees. The Milarch family faced opposition
from the start: cloning ancient trees will never meet with
success; perhaps preserving genetics is not the answer
we are looking for; David is no scientist, and there is no
precedent for such a project. David counters that a tree
alive for one thousand years may indeed know something
about survival, and he says: "These trees need to be archived, the sooner the better, and the universe wants it,
so we'll get it done." Archangel believes that redwoods
specifically are "eco-cleansing filter systems," by nature
designed to purify soil, air, and water.

David Milarch grew up with trees—his father was a shade tree nurseryman, based in Copemish. David was pushed by his father to work hard from a young age, and he pushed the limits of his own body for years; one night, after he had given up drinking—cold turkey—he suffered liver and kidney failure and was rushed to the hospital. After a near-death experience, he reentered life with a clear purpose. He had journeyed to another realm and was told by light beings that he had work to do on earth: to rescue trees. The esteemed science writer Jim Robbins uses a rather long word to describe leaving the body, an event well-documented: *disambiguation*, though perhaps more exact here would be the term coined by the French mystic and scholar Henry Corbin—David had traveled into an "imaginal realm." He shares this story freely and openly, unabashed (a word Basil Bunting favored), and his work with champion trees for three decades germinates from that transport into white light. (I must return to my chosen story, but I direct you to the excellent book by Robbins, *The Man Who Planted Trees*, for the full account).

AATA has propagated more than 300,000 trees over the past 25 years, and they project an ability to propagate more than 1 million, once funding is secured to improve infrastructure. With the aid of forestry scientists, Archangel has created a list of one hundred North American species most essential to clone. The nonprofit organization has cloned and replanted old-growth ash trees at Mount Vernon, the home of George Washington; oaks at Jefferson's Monticello; and European copper beech trees at Teddy Roosevelt's Sagamore Hill. Groves have been established in the Pacific Northwest, in Europe, and in New Zealand.

In 2018, Archangel planted saplings cloned from ancient sequoia stumps at the Presidio in San Francisco, to create a super grove. On a major expedition, AATA took cuttings from 130 of the oldest trees in Ireland—oak, holly, hazel, and yew—including a *Quercus robur* known as the Brian Boru tree. This massive oak may be 1,500 years old, and it is said that the last high king of Ireland gathered 1,000 of his men beneath its branches. With some confidence David Milarch revealed the intention of his visit to the emerald isle: "We're here to help Ireland save the last of its old growth." And to date, according to Milarch, no one has yet imagined a better solution to mitigate the effects of climate disruption.

When he was given a book by Diana Beresford-Kroeger, the respected botanist and medical biochemist, Milarch reached out to her, and in turn she offered support for the Archangel vision. Her education as a child into the Brehon Law of Ireland is interfused with her work as a twenty-first-century scientist, and her belief in the importance of tree aerosols rhymes with Milarch's intuition. She is a champion of the importance of these chemical mists emitted by trees: "These substances are at the heart of connectivity in nature." At present, Beresford-Kroeger advocates for a global bioplan to encourage every citizen to reawaken to this connectivity, most specifically to protect and to restore forests wherever possible. She claims that "the genetic information of a mother tree is perhaps the most important living library there is."

In a very confusing taxonomic reordering of the conifers, redwoods, once considered members of the Taxodiaceae family, are now included in the family Cupressaceae, the only conifer family to grow throughout the world. The trees have no identity crisis; confusion arises from our human need to classify. Only three genera of redwoods remain in existence: the coastal redwood (*Sequoia sempervirens*), the giant redwood (*Sequoiadendron giganteum*), and the dawn redwood you met in an earlier chapter (*Metasequoia glyptostroboides*). The botanical name derives from the grandson of a Cherokee chief: Sequoya, the man who invented the Cherokee alphabet. Although countless millions of people worldwide who have never encountered a redwood might disagree—and who might perhaps nominate a yew, an oak, a banyan, a baobab, or a totara—redwoods have been called the world's most loved tree. Standing beneath one—or inside one, as I have done—is truly a humbling experience. Coastal redwoods regularly reach 200 to 300 hundred feet in height, and the champion *Sequoia sempervirens* climbs to 380 feet into the air. A tree that size hosts so much diversity of life within its branches and canopy that some consider each tree an ecological zone. *Sequoiadendron*, although lesser in height, is greater in girth; the famed specimen, General Sherman, 2,700 years old and thought to be the largest living organism on the planet, weighs 1,200 tons. After so many years of rampant logging, we do not possess an accurate inventory of the champions lost to axe or saw blade and human hubris. However, DNA has been sourced from the stump remains of ancient giant sequoias to indicate the previous existence of trees significantly larger than General Sherman. On a day now known as the Day of Discovery, early May 1998, two friends, botanist Stephen C. Sillett and naturalist Michael Taylor, set off in search of some champion trees in the rainforest of Jedediah Smith Redwoods State Park, 20 miles south of the Oregon border. Toward the end of a challenging, sometimes harrowing trek, they came upon a ring of redwood titans, unreported until that day. Later, when they took care to measure a tree now known as the Lost Monarch, they discovered it was 30 feet across at the base. Collectively, the Grove of the Titans is home to the largest redwoods on planet Earth.

Redwoods have a soft, spongy bark, one foot thick on the oldest trees, resistant to most fires and insects (so far), so lightning is the prime natural threat. Native Americans traditionally set fires to diminish the understory brush, to the benefit of the trees whose cones require heat to open and release seeds. However, in the past few years, the intensity of California forest fires has had a disastrous effect on these iconic trees—it is estimated that one-fifth of the world's sequoias have been lost or damaged due to recent wildfires. Following the Windy wildfire, in 2021 AATA sent a team to the mountain community of Sequoia Crest to replant giant sequoia saplings in the fire-ravaged landscape, and they were joined by local schoolchildren in the planting. Amazingly, only two years before the fire, Archangel had taken cuttings from one of the oldest and largest of the giants, Waterfall—an elder that sadly succumbed to the blaze. Today, among the ashes, new growth rises.

Before the saplings arrived from Copemish, we visited the home of the mother trees at LongHouse Reserve with several children, to introduce them to the story; my son, a cinematographer, filmed the graceful sequoias and the equally graceful children. Seven-year-old Indie, his hands on a tall redwood, said this: "Because of climate change, the trees are dying, and if there's no trees, there's no oxygen, and if there's no oxygen, there's going to be no people."

At Hayground, we laid out a serpentine pattern that winds through the former potato field and arrives at a circle: a place to gather, a future grove. We envision that one day classes will be held here, under a canopy of redwood leaves and branches, and someone may remember the poetic thought (that began this book) of Rabindranath Tagore concerning instructor and students: of your two teachers you will gain more wisdom from the trees.

But, today, in lieu of a class, a celebration: the newly planted saplings encircle an entire school of children, teachers, former students, gardeners, the LongHouse horticulturist, sequoia lovers. Seated in the center of the circle, Becky Genia, a respected elder from the Shinnecock Nation, speaks and sings. Her words are reverent and instructive and loving toward the children. Her blessing is named the "Corn Dance Song," and eight-year-old Lucia times her rattle perfectly to Becky's drum. Calmly, one child after another speaks of this other species that we need to nurture. Within the circle, as we nest together, "we place ourselves at the origin of confidence in the world." The song lingers long in the air, we return to planting saplings, and a five-year-old child, her hands immersed in soil and roots, responds easily to Megan's question, "What do you hear the trees saying?" Her answer: "Thank you for planting us."

Epilogue

A FLASH OF BEAUTY

The word he chose to express "fragile" was filled with the intricacies of a continuing process, and with a strength inherent in spider webs woven across paths through sand hills where early in the morning the sun becomes entangled in each filament of web. It took a long time to explain the fragility and intricacy because no word exists alone, and the reason for choosing each word had to be explained with a story about why it must be said this certain way.

—LESLIE MARMON SILKO, *CEREMONY*

The bird a nest, the spider a web, man friendship.

—WILLIAM BLAKE, *PROVERBS OF HELL*

May has arrived, and I'm turning ground in the herb garden with a long-handled shovel, as I was taught on the coastal fields of Cornwall by my meadow mentor, Edgar Wallis. "Turn 'im over rough!" he would say, and his delivery matched the expression perfectly. "Let the wind and rain loosen 'im."

That way I learned the art of shovel and spade, in the hedge school, if you will—a method to prepare the ground for planting—focused on the immediate task while learning to read the soil. Now, here, in the herb garden on this other peninsula, the steel share of the shovel, after the spring rains, cuts through clay like butter. I turn it over rough, and throw the loam forward, stepping back, lifting the ash handle with my thigh just above the knee.

I stop to sip the spirit of the place—I can taste it—and words rise up out of the soil: This landscape is crisp within Earth's spin. I am surrounded by the white pines, maples, locusts, the one cherry, and the one larch I now know so well. I've planted some trees here in this garden, part of the project known as Zai Sheng (regeneration) Herbs, to learn more about the medicinal qualities of mimosa, arborvitae, *Eucommia*, liquidambar, and Sichuan pepper. In the adjacent fields to the north and south, a young crew of community farmers cultivate potatoes, garlic, and greens, as they learn to recognize true fertility in a field and what it means to labor within the cycle that Sir Albert Howard, drawing on Eastern religions, names the "Wheel of Life." Swallows turn and wheel in their dance of feeding, their cream breasts a flash of beauty against the blue. Their flight is an art that livens the air, the space between earth and the distant reach of the cosmos.

John Hay, after writing masterfully about nature for many years, revealed that he did not know what it meant. After decades of fostering a daily conversation with the natural world, I am in sympathy with Hay, but if a gesture of nature can translate what cannot be said, I have seen it—as in one past spring, when the handsome tulip tree (*Liriodendron tulipifera*) growing in place for twenty-five years in the field we call Birch Hill burst into abundant flower for the first time. My aspiration is to follow the model of the many-voiced

Portuguese poet Fernando Pessoa, who wrote, "I don't know what nature is—I sing it."

To celebrate the shapely flowers of a plant that flourished last summer in this herb garden—*Platycodon grandiflorus* (balloon flower)—I wrote this, titled "Furyu" ("wind-fluent"), after Bashō:

> Wind-fluent, balloon flowers
> pop in mist: purple
> stars wind-fluent flying!

***

> Angelica, whipped
> by wind, bows to silt loam:
> pollinators come (up or down).

***

> Flowers of the floating world
> kiss clay, silt, wheat:
> soil, too, woven by wind.

Trees have been my close companions throughout the making of this book, from the elegant beech tree that hugs the farm building in Amagansett and whose canopy envelopes it, to the red oaks, white oaks, pines, and hickories that surround my home, to tracing the lineage of *Metasequoia*, the dawn redwood, to the hardy redwood saplings that arrived this spring from Michigan. I am in full agreement with Colin Tudge, who writes in *The Tree*:

> Trees are right at the heart of all the necessary
> debates: ecological, social, economic, political,
> moral, religious . . . Trees could indeed stand at
> the heart of all the world's economics and poli-
> tics, just as they are at the center of all terrestrial
> ecology . . . In the future of humanity, and of all
> the world in all its aspects, trees are key players.

From our beginning, humans have celebrated the forces of nature—and found identity through interaction—often through rituals centered around trees. The tree of life, or universal tree, is an enduring symbol for this recipro- cal relationship. It is not surprising that so many differ- ent species are revered by various peoples as the tree of life. As Alexander von Humboldt reported, musing on the Mauritia palm in the Llanos region of Venezuela and Colombia: "We observed with astonishment . . . how many things are connected with the existence of a single plant." Andrea Wulf writes that "Humboldt has discovered the idea of a keynote species, a species that is as essential for an ecosystem as a keystone is to an arch, almost 200 years be- fore the concept was named." In concert with that concept is the unnameable aspect—the interbeing that a Mauritia palm, a baobab, a yew, an ash embodies, and out of body and spirit, mythologies are born. The tree of life, Wulf notes, is "the perfect symbol of nature as a living organ- ism." The earliest written literature we have access to, the Indian Vedas and Upanishads, link the banyan tree with Brahma, the innermost spirit of the universe.

Trees give us food, shelter, medicine, fire, and heat, and though they serve well as symbols and as metaphor, they rise or stand a priori. A growing knowledge of how some tree species are able to survive for millennia, and to communicate with one another, is instructive and heartening, even as forests worldwide are under siege.

In *The Tree Where Man Was Born*, Peter Matthiessen writes of one species honored as a tree of life, *Adansonia digitata*. The baobab is an arboreal wonder that can live for twenty-five hundred years and hold thirty thousand gallons of water on reserve within walls of wood (lifesaving in drought), and each tree can provide shelter in rains, fiber for thread, egg-shaped fruits rich in protein, and a silken green nut that can be pressed for oil and pounded into an edible paste. Baobabs have been called ancient arks of biodiversity. Man climbed down to earth from a baobab, says the Hadza tribe of northern Tanzania. The tree is perceived as a gate to the spirit world, though *Adansonia* is equally rooted in the only earth we know—the ancestral lineage can be traced back forty million years. Recently, through her exquisite photography, Beth Moon has worked to raise awareness of the need to protect and conserve this iconic species under stress due to climate disruption.

In a lyrical passage inspired by the African continent, where one feels, in the open spaces, "the sense of origins, of innocence and mystery," Matthiessen, traveler to the place where man was born, is led to view red paintings on rock, perhaps thousands of years old. Within a cave hidden in a thicket, he asks the Indigenous people—in the land of their ancestors—about the origin of the art. The Hadza reply, shyly: "How can we know?" Matthiessen, visitor from another continent (the New World), realizes that "our need to understand makes the Hadza uncomfortable."

Our need to understand—the need of our dominant culture—makes me uncomfortable too, though not our curiosity or our resolve to question. Faithkeeper Oren Lyons has this to say about our place in the natural order: "Humans exist somewhere between the mountain and the ant . . . there and only there." If human history is revealed as a succession of adventures into the unknown, we would be wise to enter the unknown with some humility, rather than hubris. As a guide, the principles of kincentric ecology—a wholistic term discussed in the work of Dennis Martinez and Enrique Salmón, "a way of relating respectfully to all life as kin and the earth as a nurturing mother"—point the way for our species to learn from the structure, the vigor, of the planet we call home. The key principles: responsibility, restraint, biodiversity enhancement, adherence to natural law, and wealth distribution.

I would add to this another key principle, a gift of life itself, something to feed on, like bread, not as an abstraction but as defined by Joy Harjo in her notes for *A Map to the Next World*: Hózhó is "beauty, beautiful—a Navajo (or Dineh) philosophical concept in which humans are recognized to be part of a harmonious system of thinking and being." Beauty is a word often used, and the meaning can sometimes be hazy, but here the word soars as a metaphor for our harmonious relation to place and those who inhabit a place. Here the word is imbedded in a map for reinhabiting our earth.

In the center of the herb plantings, a golden garden spider—also known as the writing spider—has built a web among the lively branching *Forsythia suspensa* after the delicate yellow flowers fell to earth. I wonder at the resilience of the spider's delicate thread that vibrates with the wind and flashes in the sunlight between seen and unseen, a thread almost without weight, spun out from a nearly weightless orb-weaving arachnid, yet strong enough to span the distance between forsythia branch and oak stake. This thin substance pulses with the basic energy of the universe, an energy fragile when displaced, though intricate in evolution and architecture, like words, made to ride changes in weather.

For the Indigenous people of this land, language, words, exist as primal, creative powers behind all things manifest—behind the spider, the forsythia branch, the light that plays on the gossamer thread. We are invited to listen, to receive the music, to make it new, and to harmonize. "No word exists alone." Here in the garden, language is alive within the web of ocean mist, fluent wind, and pollinators returning to brush the flowers of May, and my choice again is obvious. I grip the ash handle to turn silt and clay, and daylight fills the furrows. Under the soil, under the eternal flux, the rhizome endures.

Leaves

To my son, Levin

When wind moves you there,
to the lake water of Cumae,
Averno sounding through wood, and fate's woman,

Sibyl, who letters leaves with her words—
remember light on leaves you see in infancy,
bound in that cave, in leaf-light and shade.

When a hinge moves, tender leaves
turn to change, south or west, her letters lost
to memory, given to wind by individual chance.

But see! In that shadow and green and now light
the lost leaves you write at Cumae,
her letters that remember your life
from cave, through wind, in woods' harmony.

NOTES

A significant number of sources that remain silently present, but fail to surface in the notations, have been influential to me as an author—essential in some cases—during the course of writing *Soil and Spirit*. For the benefit of readers who may wish to continue the journey I have listed a selection of these texts, following these Notes.

PROLOGUE: A GOLDEN-FLEDGED GROWTH

1   *ever-expanding dynamic circles of connectivity*: Mary Evelyn Tucker, "From Home to Cosmos," in *Hearth*, ed. Annick Smith and Susan O'Connor (Minneapolis, MN: Milkweed Editions, 2018), 246.

1   *Part of our role here*: Gary Paul Nabhan, *Mesquite: An Arboreal Love Affair* (White River Junction, VT: Chelsea Green Publishing, 2018), 133.

3   *Often at a loss of how to proceed*: The Men of the Trees was founded in 1922 in Kenya by Richard "St. Barbe" Baker and Chief Josiah Njonjo, with a focus on restoring forests and building community. The mission remains the same one hundred years later: to "share a vision with millions of people, of a world in which trees and forests flourish and their vital role in sustaining planetary and human well-being is valued." "About us," International Tree Foundation, internationaltreefoundation. org/since-1922. St. Barbe was known as the first global conservationist, and his work—and that of the International Tree Foundation—has inspired the planting of twenty-six billion trees across the globe.

5   *miraculous that comes so close*: Peter Matthiessen, *In Paradise: A Novel* (New York: Riverhead Books, 2014), v. A line translated from a poem by the Russian poet Anna Akhmatova and chosen by Peter Matthiessen as the epigraph to his final novel.

1. INEXHAUSTIBLE WAYS OF SEEING

8   *The piglet lived*: A. A. Milne, *Pooh and Piglet Go Hunting* (London: Methuen Children's Books, 1983), 7.

10   *wood wide web*: Peter Wohlleben, *The Hidden Life of Trees: The Illustrated Edition*, ed. Jane Billinghurst (Vancouver: Greystone

Books, 2018), 20. The term, widely circulated by now, was actually coined by the English researcher David Read, in his discussions with the editor of the journal *Nature*, in 1997. This catchy phase— also accurate!—first appeared in that issue of *Nature*. Read was asked to write a commentary on the experimental work of forest ecologist Dr. Suzanne Simard, of the University of British Columbia (whom you will meet in future chapters).

10 *Achieving a relationship with nature*: John Fowles, *The Tree* (New York: Ecco, 1983), 39.

12 *Wheel of Life*: Wendell Berry, *The Collected Poems of Wendell Berry, 1957–1982* (New York: North Point Press, 1987), 231.

12 *We are living through a scientific revolution*: David R. Montgomery and Anne Biklé, *The Hidden Half of Nature: The Microbial Roots of Life and Health* (New York: W. W. Norton & Company, 2016), 1.

12 *a strange, invisible friend*: Neil DeGrasse Tyson, *Astrophysics for People in a Hurry* (New York/London: W. W. Norton & Company, 2017), 93.

14 *Evolution has turned man*: Fowles, *The Tree*, 26.

14 *as a perfect inversion of the human realm*: Robert MacFarlane, *Underland: A Deep Time Journey* (New York/London: W.W. Norton & Company, 2019), 18.

14 *lives on its rhizome*: Claire Dunne, *Carl Jung: Wounded Healer of the Soul, An Illustrated Biography* (New York: Parabola Books, 2000), 216.

14 *underneath the eternal flux*: Dunne, *Carl Jung*, 216.

15 *one of the earth's inexhaustible ways of seeing*: John Hay, *The Immortal Wilderness* (New York: W. W. Norton & Company, 1989), 179.

2. TONGUES IN TREES, BOOKS IN THE RUNNING BROOKS

17 *Every day and every moment they were talking*: Richard Erdoes and Alfonso Ortiz, eds., *American Indian Myths and Legends* (New York: Pantheon Books, 1984), 131.

18 *I was unaware that an underground social network*: Simard's paper on tree-fungus mutualism, as noted above, was groundbreaking, though originally disputed; now her work has found a wider audience and continues to be influential in multiple disciplines. In his brilliant novel *The Overstory*, Richard Powers imagines a riveting character, Patricia Westerford, thought to be modeled on Suzanne Simard and botanist and author Diana

Beresford-Kroeger. The English writer Robert MacFarlane, in his book *Underland*, praises Simard, and introduces another intriguing forest detective, the young English ecologist Merlin Sheldrake. In his own recent book *Entangled Life*, Sheldrake devotes a fascinating chapter to wood wide webs. The concept also influenced the story line of *Avatar*, by the filmmaker James Cameron.

20   *are good for other things than boards and shingles*: Richard Higgins, *Thoreau and the Language of Trees* (Oakland, CA: University of California Press, 2017), 56.

20   *something like the woodland sounds*: Higgins, *Thoreau*, 55.

20   *Who will go drive with Fergus*: W. B. Yeats, *The Collected Poems*, "Who Goes with Fergus?" (New York: The Macmillan Company, 1970), 43.

20   *Tell me, tell me, tell me, elm!*: James Joyce, *A Shorter Finnegans Wake*, ed. Anthony Burgess (New York: Viking Press, 1967), 92.

21   *mightie greate wooddes*: Eric Rutkow, *American Canopy: Trees, Forests, and the Making of a Nation* (New York: Scribner, 2012), 15.

22   *the trackless Amazonian forest*: Aldo Leopold, "The River of the Mother of God," in *The River of the Mother of God and Other Essays by Aldo Leopold*, ed. Susan L. Flader and J. Baird Callicott (Madison, WI: The University of Wisconsin Press, 1991), 123.

22   *the dawn-wind rustling in autumnal trees*: Leopold, "The River," 123.

23   *is but a succession of adventures into the Unknown*: Leopold, "The River," 124.

24   *And unlike logs cut from hardwoods*: Rutkow, *American Canopy*, 107.

24   *Upon the hills grow notable high timber trees*: Andrew M. Barton, Alan S. White, and Charles V. Cogbill, *The Changing Nature of the Maine Woods* (Durham, NH: University of New Hampshire Press, 2012), 91.

25   *We had better be without gold*: Andrea Wulf, *The Invention of Nature: Alexander von Humboldt's New World* (New York: Alfred A. Knopf, 2016), 65.

25   *reclothe the land*: Henry Hobhouse, *Seeds of Wealth: Five Plants That Made Men Rich* (Berkeley, CA: Counterpoint, 2005), 3.

25   *All human civilization and culture*: Fred Hageneder, *The Spirit of Trees: Science, Symbiosis, and Inspiration* (Edinburgh: Floris Books, 2017), 18.

25   *There is no finer tree*: Higgins, *Thoreau*, 121. Thoreau continues: "But the pine is no more lumber than man is, and to be made into boards and houses is no more its true and highest use

than the truest use of a man is to be cut down and made into manure." Higgins, *Thoreau*, 124.

26   *Zhingwaak, zhingwaak, nos sa!*: Jennifer Elise Foerster, Joy Harjo, and LeAnne Howe, eds., *When the Light of the World Was Subdued, Our Songs Came Through: A Norton Anthology of Native Nations Poetry* (New York: W. W. Norton & Company, 2020), 21.

27   *Man has too long forgotten*: Rutkow, *American Canopy*, 246.

27   *the right of enjoying the use*: *The Compact Oxford English Dictionary*, 2nd ed. (1991), s.v. "usufruct."

28   *relearning, recentering, returning*: First Light (website), firstlightlearningjourney.net.

28   *But trees—or, more appropriately, forests*: Chelsea Steinauer-Scudder and Jeremy Seifert, "They Carry Us with Them: The Great Tree Migration," *Emergence Magazine*, 2022, emergencemagazine.org/feature/they-carry-us-with-them.

29   *Poetry, like music, is to be heard*: Basil Bunting, *Collected Poems*, London: Fulcrum Press, 1970), back cover quotation.

30   *"In making the handle*: Gary Snyder, *Axe Handles: Poems* (Washington, DC: Shoemaker & Hoard, 2005), 6.

31   *My grained ash an hundred times hath broke*: William Shakespeare, *Coriolanus*, ed. G. Blakemore Evans (Boston: Houghton Mifflin Company, 1974), 4.5.107–108. References are to act, scene, and line.

31   *to have a spirit, or to be alive*: Enrique Salmón, *Iwígara: The Kinship of Plants and People* (Portland, OR: Timber Press, 2020), 26.

32   *It is more likely that the sky god*: Known by multiple peoples and cultures alternately as "the tree of life," "the world tree," or "the cosmic tree," many different species have been worshipped, celebrated, and mythologized for as long as trees and humans have shared the earth. This theme, like roots, branches, buds, and leaves, is gestural throughout this book.

32   *Well-being I won*: Ralph H. Blum, *The Book of Runes, 25th Anniversary Edition* (New York: St. Martin's Press, 2008), 11.

33   *the accurate transmission of feeling*: Louis Zukofsky, *A Test of Poetry* (New York: Jargon/Corinth Books, 1964), 63.

34   *Well, you know or don't you*: Joyce, *A Shorter Finnegans Wake*, 89.

35   *We are the stars who sing*: Glenn Welker, "Abenaki Literature," Indigenous Peoples Literature, indigenouspeople.net/abnaki.htm.

3. A CARE FOR WORDS

37   *Let's begin with heather*: Ogham (pronounced *OO-am*, or possibly *OG-am*) is considered one of the early alphabets of Europe, possibly dating from the first century. Each letter is named for a tree or a plant companion. The "song of the universe" was gifted in the form of script to young Ogma (the Irish god of literature and eloquence), and it reads as a synthesis of ancient story, forest, and people. Appropriately the first letters of Ogham were inscribed on the bark of aspen and hazel, later carved into standing stone markers. The characters, or letters, were known as *feda* (trees) or *nin* (forking branches). (It was a forking branch I took, to Kilkenny, on my journey to the west of Ireland.) The letters of the alphabet grow from the ground like a tree—the branches that signify sound are scratched onto the upward thrust of the tree's central body. Katie Holten, an Irish artist, seems to have inherited the spirit that moved the maker of Ogham; she recently created her own Irish Tree Alphabet that translates into a love for the wild and the whole of the natural world.

37   *Still keeps the Ling its darksome green*: John Clare, *The Shepherd's Calendar; with Village Stories, and Other Poems* (London: James Duncan, 1827), 193.

38   *Heathland is one last memory*: Diana Beresford-Kroeger, *To Speak for the Trees: My Life's Journey from Ancient Celtic Wisdom to a Healing Vision of the Forest* (Toronto: Random House Canada, 2019), 274.

38   *And some time make the time to drive out west*: Seamus Heaney, *The Spirit Level: Poems* (New York: Farrar, Straus and Giroux, 2014), 82.

40   *What made me live*: W. B. Yeats, *Stream and Sun at Glendalough: The Collected Poems*, 250.

40   *as rare as hen's teeth*: Beresford-Kroeger, *To Speak*, 275.

41   *The gunwale's lifting ear*: Seamus Heaney, *Field Work: Poems* (New York: Farrar, Straus and Giroux, 1979), 29.

42   *Decades later, the red felt-tip script*: In "Digging," the first poem of his first published book, Heaney draws a parallel between the "squat pen" that rests in his own hand and his father's spade. I know the analogy well, and feel it "deep in both our weights."

42   *peasant stock*: Eugène Guillevic, John Montague (trans.), *Carnac* (Hexham, Northumberland: Bloodaxe Books, 1999), 9.

43   *Who but I*: Ithell Colquhoun, *The Living Stones: Cornwall*, "Song of Amergin," (London and Chicago: Peter Owen, 2018), epigraph.

43　*That which is not in stone*: Eugène Guillevic, *Guillevic: Selected Poems*, ed. Denise Levertov (New York: New Directions, 1969), 45.

44　*Guillevic referred to himself*: In a prose poem entitled "Seers?" Guillevic wrote: "For poets there is a road that must be travelled in order to arrive at living on the true side of life, that side of it one can finally affirm, that side of it that so far is seen only in exceptional moments and in particular during the reading or writing of a poem." Guillevic, *Guillevic*, 3.

44　*the rest is proper breathing space*: Zukofsky, *A Test of Poetry*, 81.

44　*Poetry and music are both patterns*: Peter Makin, ed., *Basil Bunting on Poetry* (Baltimore, MD: The Johns Hopkins University Press, 1999), 4.

45　*The moment is dear to us*: Stanley Kunitz, *Passing Through: The Later Poems, New and Selected* (New York: W. W. Norton & Company, 1995), 11.

45　*Between heather and marigold*: Seamus Heaney, *Human Chain: Poems* (New York: Farrar, Straus and Giroux, 2010), 43.

46　*Mer. Mer au bord du neant*: Guillevic, *Carnac*, 30.

46　*earthed lightning*: Seamus Heaney, *The Spirit Level: Poems*, 82.

4. IN THE SEASON OF GRAIN RAIN

49　*consciousness as empty awareness*: David Hinton, trans., *Mountain Home: The Wilderness Poetry of Ancient China* (New York: New Directions, 2005), 281.

49　*And at this fundamental level*: Hinton, *Mountain Home*, 281.

50　*When the vein of jade*: Lu Chi, Sam Hamill, trans., *The Art of Writing* (Minneapolis: Milkweed Editions, 2000), 22.

50　*cascades tumbling a hundred Ways*: Hinton, *Mountain Home*, 238.

50　*Water rinses my feet*: Hinton, *Mountain Home*, 240.

51　*Would you be willing to identify*: My own retelling of the story, from various sources.

51　*There must be a god in the tree*: LAM Staff, "The Metasequoia Mystery," *Landscape Architecture Magazine*, January 19, 2016, landscapearchitecturemagazine.org/2016/01/19/the-metasequoia-mystery.

53　*Here was a fossil come to life*: "How UC – Berkeley prof saved dawn redwoods," *Coronado Eagle & Journal*, May 22, 1969.

54　*Old master Tsung*: Lu Chi, *The Art of Writing*, xxxii.

54　*The poet stands at the center of the universe*: Lu Chi, *The Art of Writing*, 6.

55   *The window / Frames the western mountains*: Kenneth Rexroth,
      One Hundred Poems from the Chinese (New York: New
      Directions, 1971), 26.

57   *learn to be a peasant in America*: Caroline Merrifield and Shi Yan,
      "CSA in China: An Introduction," Urgenci, urgenci.net/csa-
      in-china-an-introduction-by-caroline-merrifield-and-shi-yan.

57   *Change won't be fast*: Katrina Yu, "Meet the woman
      leading China's new organic farming army," Al Jazeera,
      November 25, 2015, aljazeera.com/features/2015/11/25/
      meet-the-woman-leading-chinas-new-organic-farming-army.

58   *Through Via Campesina, an international peasant movement*: "Food
      sovereignty is the right of peoples to healthy and culturally
      appropriate food produced through ecologically sound and
      sustainable methods, and their right to define their own food
      and agriculture systems. It puts those who produce, distribute
      and consume food at the heart of food systems and policies
      rather than the demands of markets and corporations. It
      defends the interests and inclusion of the next generation. It
      offers a strategy to resist and dismantle the current corporate
      trade and food regime, and directions for food, farming,
      pastoral and fisheries systems determined by local producers.
      Food sovereignty prioritises local and national economies and
      markets and empowers peasant and family farmer-driven
      agriculture, artisanal-fishing, pastoralist-led grazing, and
      food production, distribution and consumption based on
      environmental, social and economic sustainability." https://
      viacampesina.org/en/food-sovereignty-a-manifesto-for-the-
      future-of-our-planet-la-via-campesina/.

59   *a countryman, rustic, a worker on the land*: *The Compact Oxford English
      Dictionary*, 2nd ed. (1991), s.v. "peasant."

59   *one of a class of persons*: *The Random House Dictionary of the English
      Language*, 2nd ed. (1987), s.v. "peasant."

59   *in the course of building its identity*: Prof. Wen Tiejun, "New Rural
      Regeneration in Contemporary China," *Touching the Heart
      Taking Root: CSA in Hong Kong, Taiwan & Mainland China* (Hong
      Kong: Partnerships for Community Development, 2015), 118.

60   *The most important raison d'être of China*: Prof. Zhang Heqing,
      "Guard the Community and Carry Out a Revolution Effected
      in Everyday Life," *Touching the Heart Taking Root: CSA in Hong*

Kong, Taiwan & Mainland China (Partnerships for Community Development, 2015), 95–98.

60   *CSA is about relationship*: As noted in conversation.

61   *But if you mount the source of heaven and earth*: Hinton, *Mountain Home*, 276.

61   *Only after looking and listening closely*: Lu Chi, *The Art of Writing*, 31.

63   *In our time, it is all but impossible*: Sam Hamill, preface to *The Art of Writing: Lu Chi's Wen Fu* (Minneapolis, MN: Milkweed Editions, 2000). In fact, unknown to me at the time, my sympathies actually align with the thinking of Ai Weiwei's father, Ai Qing, China's most renowned twentieth-century poet. In 1938 he wrote a piece entitled *On Poetry*: "Poetry today ought to be a bold experiment in the democratic spirit . . . A constitution matters even more to poets than to others, because only when the right to expression is guaranteed can one give voice to the hopes of people at large . . . To suppress the voices of the people is the cruelest form of violence." Orville Schell, "The Uncompromising Ai Weiwei," *New York Review of Books*, March 10, 2022, nybooks.com/articles/2022/03/10/the-uncompromising-ai-weiwei.

65   *to abide by the laws of nature*: Partnerships for Community Development, *Touching the Heart Taking Root*, 18.

65   *When roots grow from nong, life thrives*: Partnerships for Community Development, *Touching the Heart Taking Root*, 19.

66   *they still follow the original practice*: Taken from a flyer given to me by the visitors from Qinghai Hainan, where three generations of Tashi families have raised bees. "According to Tashi's father's words, they kowtow toward the snow-capped mountains and pray to God everyday except rainy or snowy days."

66   *They also gifted me a delicate folded package*: Appropriate here is a passage from David Hinton's magnificent biography of Tu Fu, *Awakened Cosmos*: "Heaven's loom of origins . . . is a mythological account describing that origin-place where language/poem, thoughts/identity, and Cosmos arise together." David Hinton, *Awakened Cosmos: The Mind of Classical Chinese Poetry* (Boulder, CO: Shambhala Publications, 2019), 69.

67   *Luminous words are brought down*: Lu Chi, *The Art of Writing*, 9.

5. OLDER THAN THOUGHT

70   *West Penwith is granite*: Colquhoun, *The Living Stones: Cornwall*, 57.

71   *Who but I*: Colquhoun, *The Living Stones: Cornwall*, epigraph.

71   *In ancient belief, stones were the bones*: Howard Mansfield, *The Bones of the Earth* (Berkeley, CA: Counterpoint, 2006), 39.

71   *It is old, Celtic*: Jane Costin, "Lawrence's 'Best Adventures': Blood-Consciousness and Cornwall," *Études Lawrenciennes* 43 (2021): 151–72, doi.org/10.4000/lawrence.95.

72   *the roots of these rocks are French*: Ian Sample, "Cornwall and south Devon 'originally part of mainland Europe,'" *The Guardian*, September 14, 2018, theguardian.com/science/2018/sep/14/cornwall-and-south-devon-originally-belonged-to-europe.

72   *Am I in France?*: Shakespeare, *King Lear*, IV, VII, 74.

72   *Mankind's mischief . . . which disturbs nature's order*: Valorie Grace Hallinan, "The Invention of Nature," *Books Can Save a Life*, November 16, 2017, bookscansavealife.com/2017/11/16/the-invention-of-nature.

73   *The place was absolutely howling*: Peter Perry, personal correspondence with author, April 29, 2020.

77   *'druid silence' of the sea*: Edna O'Brien, "James Joyce's Odyssey," *The New Yorker*, May 30, 1999, newyorker.com/magazine/1999/06/07/joyces-odyssey.

78   *then off, off forth on swing*: Gerard Manley Hopkins, "The Windhover," *A Hopkins Reader*, John Pick (ed.), (Garden City: Image Books, 1966), 50.

79   *for the lonely places where physical danger*: Andrew Lanyon, *Peter Lanyon: 1918–1964* (Penzance, UK: Andrew Lanyon, 1990), 223.

79   *His imagination was agile, even elastic*: Lanyon, *Peter Lanyon*, 9.

79   *I got the smell of paint very early*: Lanyon, *Peter Lanyon*, 23.

79   *Remember, there are thousands of tons of weight there*: Lanyon, *Peter Lanyon*, 24.

80   *Doodling—in space*: Lanyon, *Peter Lanyon*, 292.

80   *the region of vertigo*: Lanyon, *Peter Lanyon*, 229.

80   *the land blowing like tossed corn*: Lanyon, *Peter Lanyon*, 156.

81   *As the painter glides over the earth*: In 1961, Peter Lanyon was elected as a bard of the Cornish Gorsedd for his services to Cornish art. His bardic name was Marghak an Gwyns, "Rider of the Winds."

81   *blue-bleak embers*: Hopkins, "The Windhover," 50.

82   *Above all there was the sensation of moving*: Barbara Hepworth, *Some Statements by Barbara Hepworth* (St Ives, UK: Barbara Hepworth Museum, 1977), 1.

82   *No sculpture really lives*: Rachel Smith, "Figure and Landscape: Barbara Hepworth's Phenomenology of Perception," *Tate Papers*, tate.org.uk/research/tate-papers/20/figure-and-landscape-barbara-hepworths-phenomenology-of-perception.

83   *Here is the time for the sayable*: Rainer Maria Rilke, *Ahead of All Parting: The Selected Poetry and Prose of Rainer Maria Rilke* (New York: Modern Library, 2015), 385.

83   *I could write a book about the crystal*: Smith, "Figure and Landscape."

84   *The inward gates of a bird are always open*: MacDiarmid, "from 'On a Raised Beach,'" Poetry Foundation, https://www.poetryfoundation.org/poems/46799/on-a-raised-beach.

84   *Always open, far longer open*: MacDiarmid, "from 'On a Raised Beach.'"

85   *told lovelier, more dangerous*: Hopkins, "The Windhover," 50.

6. CULTURA

88   *We are, at the most basic level*: David Quammen, *The Tangled Tree: A Radical New History of Life* (New York: Simon & Schuster, 2018), 76.

89   *Over the past two billion or so years*: Colin Tudge, *The Tree: A Natural History of What Trees Are, How They Live, and Why They Matter* (New York: Three Rivers Press, 2005), 61.

89   *This is no flattery*: William Shakespeare, *As You Like It*, ed. G. Blakemore Evans (Boston: Houghton Mifflin Company, 1974), 2.1.10–11. References are to act, scene, and line.

89   *There is a planetary emergency*: "About our mission," Eden Project, edenproject.com/mission/about-our-mission.

90   *Our clay-dumps are converging on the land*: Jack Clemo, *Selected Poems* (Northumberland, UK: Bloodaxe Books, 1988), 25.

91   *the great white conical heaps*: Bernard Leach, *A Potter's Book* (London: Faber & Faber, 1973), 44.

92   *The natural decomposition of granite*: Leach, *A Potter's Book*, 44.

93   *We had flesh and blood in mind*: Tim Smit, *The Lost Gardens of Heligan* (London: Seven Dials, 2017), 50.

95   *the creation and exercise of wonder*: Leopold, "The River of the Mother of God," 276.

95   *the world's first ecological book*: Wulf, *The Invention of Nature*, 127.

95   *In 1866, the German zoologist Ernst Haeckel*: I invite you to read of
     Ernst Haeckel, who cofounded a magazine to honor the work
     of Humboldt and Darwin titled *Kosmos*, in Andrea Wulf's lively
     book *The Invention of Nature*. His drawings of radiolarians—
     minuscule single-celled sea organisms, "sea wonders"—and
     medusae (jellyfish), are truly dazzling. After identifying more
     than a hundred new species, he published a book titled *Die
     Radiolarien (Rhizopoda radiaria)*.

95   *changed, changed utterly*: W. B. Yeats, *The Collected Poems*, "Easter
     1916," 178.

96   *As the pall of eternal slumber*: Smit, *The Lost Gardens of Heligan*, 74.

96   *the Eden Project celebrates*: "Our mission: plants and nature,"
     Eden Project, edenproject.com/mission/about-our-mission/
     our-mission-plants-and-nature.

97   *We have left our Edenic Pleistocene heritage*: Jack Loeffler,
     "Restoring Indigenous Mindfulness within the Commons of
     Human Consciousness," in *What Kind of Ancestor Do You Want
     to Be?*, eds. John Hausdoerffer, Brooke Parry Hecht, Melissa
     K. Nelson, and Katherine Kassouf Cummings (Chicago: The
     University of Chicago Press, 2021), 136.

100 *If some small but critical mass*: Richard Powers, *Bewilderment: A
     Novel* (New York: W. W. Norton & Company, 2021), 177.

101 *the beverage of the friends of God*: https://quozio.com/
     quote/77672b9a/1025/o-coffee-thou-dost-dispel-all-care-thou-
     are-the-object-of.

102 *We are an educational charity*: "Eden's Mission," Eden Project,
     edenproject.com/mission.

103 *of the earth's inexhaustible ways of seeing*: Hay, *The Immortal
     Wilderness*, 179.

103 *Plants at Eden are a metaphor*: Tim Smit, *Eden: Updated 15th
     Anniversary Edition* (Bodelva, UK: Eden Project, 2016), 163.

104 *was built on a trust ticket*: Smit, *Eden*, 273.

104 *Culture, Tim reminds us*: To take the thought further I will add
     these words of the anthropologist Edward T. Hall, recorded
     by aural historian Jack Loeffler: "Culture is an extension
     of the genetic code. In other words, we are part of Nature
     ourselves . . . The evolution of our species really depends on
     not developing our technology but developing our spirits or our

souls. The fact is that Nature is so extraordinarily complex that you can look at it from multiple dimensions, and come up with very different answers, and each one of them will be true. And we need all of those truths." Loeffler, "Restoring Indigenous Mindfulness," 135.

104   *a cultural archive of trees*: "Info," Folly Tree Arboretum, follytreearboretum.com/about-visit.

105   *The figures are floating, like reflections*: Diane Waldman, *William De Kooning* (London: Thames and Hudson, 1988), 136.

106   *promote an exuberant environmental ethic*: "Info," Folly Tree Arboretum.

107   *cylinder of living cells*: Peter Crane, *Ginkgo: The Tree That Time Forgot* (New Haven, CT: Yale University Press, 2013), 48.

108   *an elephant fruit in a land*: Connie Barlow, "Anachronistic Fruits and the Ghosts Who Haunt Them," *Arnoldia* 61, no. 2 (July 15, 2001), arboretum.harvard.edu/stories/ anachronistic-fruits-and-the-ghosts-who-haunt-them.

109   *after dinner, the weather being warm*: "Revised Memoir of Newton," The Newton Project, published online September 2004, newtonproject.ox.ac.uk/view/texts/normalized/OTHE00001.

111   *Wherever the art of medicine is loved*: Hippocrates, https://www. goodreads.com/quotes/22447-wherever-the-art-of-medicine-is-loved-there-is-also.

111   *For and in consideration of the great love*: "The Tree That Owns Itself," Athens Georgia (website), https://www.visitathensga. com/listing/the-tree-that-owns-itself/234/.

112   *Should trees have standing?*: Richard Powers, *The Overstory: A Novel* (New York: W. W. Norton & Company, 2018), 249.

112   *a wall-less single celled organism*: "Witches' broom," Missouri Botanical Garden (website), https://www. missouribotanicalgarden.org/gardens-gardening/your-garden/help-for-the-home-gardener/advice-tips-resources/ pests-and-problems/diseases/witches-broom.

113   *In spite of all the history*: Leah Bayens, "Interview: Wendell Berry," in *What Kind of Ancestor Do You Want to Be?*, eds. John Hausdoerffer, Brooke Parry Hecht, Melissa K. Nelson, and Katherine Kassouf Cummings (Chicago: The University of Chicago Press, 2021), 39.

7. A STRONG SONG

115 *There seemed nothing to do*: Basil Bunting, trans., *Bunting's Persia*, ed. Don Share (Chicago: Flood Editions, 2012), xi.

116 *Years later, while serving in the Royal Air Force*: Since 1000 BC this land, at one time part of the greatest empire in the world, has been known by many names: Arya, Iran, Iranshahr, Iranzamin . . . though Persia was long the accepted choice of the Western world. In 1935, the government of Reza Shah Pahlavi requested that other nations use Iran—"land of the Aryans"—as the official chosen name.

116 *Along the way he was a conscientious objector*: Richard Burton, *A Strong Song Tows Us: The Life of Basil Bunting* (Oxford: Infinite Ideas, 2013), 1.

116 *Binghamton was a dreadful climate*: Burton, *A Strong Song Tows Us*, 441.

117 *like oxen*: Burton, *A Strong Song Tows Us*, 440.

117 *An adoring guide I would say*: In one of so many letters I received from Milt he wrote: "Basil was historical, sceptical, erotic, insolent—as well as extremely beautiful! Also international." Milton Kessler, personal correspondence with author, January 1989.

118 *an autobiography, but not a record of fact*: Bunting, *Collected Poems*, 156.

118 *Brief words are hard to find*: Bunting, *Collected Poems*, 54.

118 *Those fail who try to force*: Basil Bunting, *A Note on Briggflatts* (Durham, UK: Basil Bunting Poetry Archive, 1989), 1.

118 *each pebble its part*: Bunting, *Collected Poems*, 51.

119 *raspy, deep, purring, falling like water*: Lisa Kenner, "The Mouse and the Lion," in *Conjunctions 8*, ed. Bradford Morrow (February 28, 2001), 205.

119 *It is time to consider how Domenico Scarlatti*: Bunting, *Collected Poems*, 66.

119 *knotty wood hard to rive*: Bunting, *Collected Poems*, 53.

119 *sycamore seed twirling*: Bunting, *Collected Poems*, 64.

119 *gleams like a berry*: Bunting, *Collected Poems*, 59.

120 *never a boast*: Bunting, *Collected Poems*, 66.

120 *no longer felt to be relevant*: Robert MacFarlane, *Landmarks* (New York: Penguin Books, 2016), 3.

120 *a kind of word magic*: MacFarlane, *Landmarks*, 4.

120 *to enchant our relations with nature*: MacFarlane, *Landmarks*, 4.

121 *Words! / Pens are too light*: Bunting, *Collected Poems*, 53.

121 *When Gunnar was ready to leave*: From a class handout, Rhetoric 158—Form and Theory.

122 *A poet must write by ear*: Bunting, *Basil Bunting on Poetry*, 36.

122 *since the poetry is in the sound*: Bunting, *Basil Bunting on Poetry*, 158.

123 *learned meter by listening*: Susan Brind Morrow, *The Names of Things: A Passage in the Egyptian Desert* (New York: Riverhead Books, 1997), 22.

123 *I like the common eye*: Basil Bunting, *The Poems of Basil Bunting*, ed. Don Share (London: Faber & Faber, 2016), 30.

123 *Take the plainest words*: Bunting, *Basil Bunting on Poetry*, 180.

123 *And I cannot have been more than eight*: Bunting, *Basil Bunting on Poetry*, 200.

124 *a splendid race*: Burton, *A Strong Song Tows Us*, 277.

124 *you could learn almost anything*: Share, *The Poems of Basil Bunting*, 532.

125 *nobody took the slightest notice of me*: Burton, *A Strong Song Tows Us*, 326.

125 *should trim some known thought*: Share, *The Poems of Basil Bunting*, 419.

125 *If ever I learned the trick of it*: Bunting, *Collected Poems*, preface.

126 *to get them in the right order*: Share, *The Poems of Basil Bunting*, 418.

127 *All things are made of atoms*: Priyamvada Natarajan, "All Things Great and Small," *New York Review of Books*, July 1, 2021, nybooks.com/articles/2021/07/01/all-things-great-and-small.

127 *All things are made of elementary particles*: Natarajan, "All Things Great and Small."

127 *So I insist that there are invisible particles*: Lucretius, *On the Nature of Things*, trans. Martin Ferguson Smith (Indianapolis, IN: Hackett Publishing Company, 2001), 11.

127 *ultimate particles*: Lucretius, *On the Nature of Things*, 4.

127 *the seeds of things*: Lucretius, *On the Nature of Things*, 4.

127 *a midwife to modernity*: Stephen Greenblatt, *The Swerve: How the World Became Modern* (New York: W. W. Norton & Company, 2011), 13.

129 *that honeyed drop of Venus' sweetness*: Lucretius, *On the Nature of Things*, 129.

129 *Find our mortal world enough*: W. H. Auden, "Lullaby," in *Collected Poems*, ed. Edward Mendelson (Toronto: Vintage International, 1991), 158.

129 *teased so much by people*: Bunting, *A Note on Briggflatts*, 1.

129 *Amongst philosophers I have most sympathy*: Bunting, *A Note on Briggflatts*, 3.

129 *No poem is profound*: Bunting, *A Note on Briggflatts*, 2.

129 *deft earth*: Bunting, *Collected Poems*, 135.

130 *Now the year ages*: Bunting, *Collected Poems*, 67.

8. JUANA'S ORANGE, ELENA'S RED

133 *the mountains affect the climate*: David Muench and Tony Hillerman, *New Mexico* (Portland, OR, C. H. Belding, 1974), 33.

134 *mind, heart, and in the spirit*: Tewa Women United (website), tewawomanunited.org.

134 *As Pueblo/Tewa women our source of strength*: "Tewa Women United Today," Tewa Women United (website), https:// tewawomenunited.org/tewa-women-united-today.

138 *is the law of life*: Kathleen Dean Moore and Michael P. Nelson, eds., *Moral Ground: Ethical Action for a Planet in Peril* (San Antonio, TX: Trinity University Press, 2010), 43.

138 *Seeds are a place and a product*: Garden's Edge (website), gardensedge.org.

138 *have been on the receiving end*: Rigoberto Quemé Chay, "The Corn Men Have Not Forgotten Their Ancient Gods," in *Environment: An Interdisciplinary Anthology*, eds. Glenn Adelson, James Engell, Brent Ranalli, and K. P. Van Anglen, (New Haven, CT: Yale University Press, 2008), 851.

138 *This great civilization, which arose*: In *Zero: The Biography of a Dangerous Idea*, Charles Seife identifies the heart of the "problem" of zero: it refuses to get bigger, it has no substance. Though many cultures have ignored or feared the concept of zero, in Mayan cosmology zero is a substance equal to the life force: it is depicted as a seed. The poet Margaret Randall invokes the shape of the Mayan number:

> as a resting oval with small curved lines,
> one on top two at the bottom,
> coming together in points at either end.
> Three shorter lines
> rise within like eyelashes or tiny sails.

The glyph is a leaf, a seed, an eye but not only.
Margaret Randall, *The Rhizome as a Field of Broken Bones: New Poems* (San Antonio, TX: Wings Press, 2013), 88.

138 *Mayas believe that all nature is life*: Chay, "The Corn Men," 851.

139 *We are not faced with two separate crises*: Pope Francis, *Laudato Si': On Care for Our Common Home* (Huntington, IN: Our Sunday Visitor, 2015), 94.

140 *the right of peoples, communities, and countries to define*: Jack

Kittredge, "Indigenous Perspectives on Food Sovereignty,"
The Natural Farmer, thenaturalfarmer.org/article/
indigenous-perspectives-on-food-soverignty.

141 *In the* Popol Vuh, *the creator*: There is a most accessible retelling
of this creation story to be found in the chapter titled "People
of Corn, People of Light," in Robin Wall Kimmerer, *Braiding
Sweetgrass*: "These people of corn are the ones who were
respectful and grateful for the world that sustained them—
and so they were the people who were sustained upon the
earth." Robin Wall Kimmerer, "People of the Corn, People
of the Light," in *Braiding Sweetgrass: Indigenous Wisdom, Scientific
Knowledge, and the Teachings of Plants* (Minneapolis, MN:
Milkweed Editions, 2013), 343.

143 *an ecology of the heart*: Gary Paul Nabhan, *Enduring Seeds: Native
American Agriculture and Wild Plant Conservation* (Tucson, AZ: The
University of Arizona Press, 1989), 84.

143 *Their native agricultures continue today*: Nabhan, *Enduring Seeds*, 83.

143 *smaller than a grain of rice*: Given the title of this book, I must draw
your attention to the stanzas of the *Chandogya Upanishad* (Muktika
canon, #9 Upanishad) that begin: "There is a Spirit which is
mind and life, light and truth and vast spaces" (3:14:2-4).

9. THE REMEMBERED EARTH

147 *Attention is the doorway to gratitude*: Maria Popova, "Gardening
and the Secret of Happiness," *The Marginalia*, themarginalian.
org/2016/02/29/robin-wall-kimmerer-braiding-sweetgrass.

148 *odor . . . and the sight and touch*: Rick Bass, "The Larch," *Orion*,
September/October 2012, 82.

148 *their magnificent and rotting bodies*: Bass, "The Larch," 82.

149 *Our trees are living history*: Rutkow, *American Canopy*, 345.

149 *My* Oxford English Dictionary *lists a weed*: My friend Carol
Williams writes: "In the early days of gardening, a retreat from
wilderness, the whole point of gardening was to grow only what
the gardener intended. Many gardeners today still feel that
way . . . Other gardeners see their gardens as an interplay between
what they intend and what nature interjects; such gardens
tolerate, even welcome, some visitors from the weed world." Carol
Williams, *Bringing a Garden to Life* (New York: Bantam Books,
1998), 114.

149 *herbaceous plant not valued*: The Compact Oxford English Dictionary, 2nd ed. (1991), s.v. "weed."

150 *In case of a famine*: Tamara Dean, "Stalking the Wild Groundnut," *Orion*, November/December 2007, 44.

151 *like beads on a necklace*: Dean, "Stalking the Wild Groundnut," 44.

151 *golden nugget . . . would be a benefit*: Dean, "Stalking the Wild Groundnut," 48.

152 *like to be alone*: Dean, "Stalking the Wild Groundnut," 46.

154 *The phoenix is rising*: "About Us," High Falls Gardens, highfallsgardens.net/aboutus/restoration.html.

155 *As the global herb community*: Peg Schafer, *The Chinese Medicinal Herb Farm: A Cultivator's Guide to Small-Scale Organic Herb Production* (White River Junction, VT: Chelsea Green Publishing, 2011), 70.

157 *The absolute meets the relative*: Peter Matthiessen and Peter Cunningham, *Are We There Yet?: A Zen Journey Through Space and Time* (Berkeley, CA: Counterpoint, 2010), 153.

157 *the earth's inexhaustible ways of seeing*: Hay, *The Immortal Wilderness*, 179.

157 *smaller than a grain of mustard seed*: Chandogya Upanishad, 3:14:3.

159 *The fabric is whole and strong*: Donald Culross Peattie, *Flowering Earth* (San Antonio, TX: Trinity University Press, 2013), 239.

10. GRAINS OF A GREAT WEB

166 *From the west windows of my house*: Peter Matthiessen, *The Wind Birds: Shorebirds of North America* (Shelbourne, Vermont: Chapters Publishing, 1994), 17.

166 *I can imagine Matthiessen's engagement*: When Matthiessen visited Aldo Leopold's shack in Sand County, he was told by Nina Leopold Bradley, Aldo's daughter, that it was the sandhill crane that made her father "an impassioned advocate of conservation." (Peter Matthiessen, *The Birds of Heaven: Travel with Cranes* [Vancouver: Greystone Books, 2001], 262.) I too visited Leopold's shack—I sat under a great pine tree, and a few needles that fell from the upper limbs into my small leather notebook are still lodged there. As his words are lodged in my memory: "A thing is right when it tends to support the integrity, the stability, and the beauty of the biotic community.

It is wrong when it tends otherwise." (Aldo Leopold, *A Sand County Almanac: And Sketches Here and There* [New York: Oxford University Press, 1949], 224.)

167 *The Trojans went forth with a cry*: Morrow, *The Names of Things*, 88.

167 *we hear the trumpet in the orchestra*: Matthiessen, *The Birds of Heaven*, xi.

167 *Their annual return*: Matthiessen, *The Birds of Heaven*, vii.

168 *One way to grasp the main perspectives*: Matthiessen, *The Birds of Heaven*, xv.

170 *Fungi are everywhere*: Merlin Sheldrake, *Entangled Life: How Fungi Make Our Worlds, Change Our Minds & Shape Our Futures* (New York: Random House, 2020), 3.

172 *Any thing reticulated or decussated*: "Some Definitions / Definitions from Johnson's Dictionary," The Samuel Johnson Sound Bite Page, samueljohnson.com/definitions. html. Johnson's entry for *lexicographer* is worth repeating: "Lexicographer: 'A writer of dictionaries; a harmless drudge, that busies himself in tracing the original, and detailing the signification of words.'" David Crystal, "Johnson's *Dictionary*: Myths and realities," British Library, June 21, 2018, bl.uk/restoration-18th-century-literature/articles/johnsons-dictionary-myths-and-realities.

172 *an intricately woven rug*: Suzanne Simard, *Finding the Mother Tree: Discovering the Wisdom of the Forest* (New York: Alfred A. Knopf, 2021), 168.

172 *There is an intricate and vast system*: Simard, *Finding the Mother Tree*, 283.

172 *I have come full circle*: Simard, *Finding the Mother Tree*, 283.

172 *the ultimate mutualism*: Sheldrake, *Entangled Life*, 125. Ecologist and writer Tom Wessels reveals his favorite example of mutualism—between the bull-horn acacia tree and the acacia ant of Mexico and Central America. The ants hollow out the swollen thorns of the acacia to create dwellings, and they feed on sap that wells on the leaf stems of the tree—they absorb protein and lipids from the acacia's leaf margins. The ants will not allow invasive vines to take hold of *their* tree, and they will defoliate any encroaching plants. Acacia ants also have an extremely venomous bite that serves to discourage herbivores searching for food. Neither tree nor resident ants can survive without the other.

172 *Symbiosis is a ubiquitous feature*: Sheldrake, *Entangled Life*, 17.

173 *a complex tangle of relationships*: Sheldrake, *Entangled Life*, 18.

173 *Am I an organism, or a community*: Daniel Dennett, *Darwin's Dangerous Idea: Evolution and the Meanings of Life* (New York: Simon & Schuster, 1995), 457.

173 *the impulse to classify organisms*: Quammen, *The Tangled Tree*, 283.

173 *I think*: Quammen, *The Tangled Tree*, 283.

173 *will aid us in understanding*: Charles Darwin, *On the Origin of Species: A Facsimile of the First Edition* (Cambridge, MA: Harvard University Press, 2001), 116.

173 *Whether or not there is a tree of life*: Quammen, *The Tangled Tree*, 308.

174 *coral of life*: Sheldrake, *Entangled Life*, 252.

174 *an elaborate bit of macramé*: Sheldrake, *Entangled Life*, 252.

174 *But 'tis a single Hair*: Emily Dickinson, *The Complete Poems of Emily Dickinson*, ed. Thomas H. Johnson (New York: Little, Brown and Company, 1960), 321.

174 *A Cobweb—wove in Adamant*: As a variation on the theme it is appropriate to include in the discussion these lines from Basil Bunting: "Applewood, hard to rive, / its knots smoulder all day. / Cobweb hair on the morning, / a puff would blow it away." Bunting, "Briggflatts," *Collected Poems*, 66.

175 *a new poster organism for evolution*: Sheldrake, *Entangled Life*, 252.

176 *changed the face of the planet*: Sheldrake, *Entangled Life*, 75.

176 *a metabolic 'song'*: Sheldrake, *Entangled Life*, 125.

177 *reciprocal alchemy*: Simard, *Finding the Mother Tree*, 176.

177 *Within eukaryotic cells*: Sheldrake, *Entangled Life*, 82.

177 *one of the most beautiful ideas*: Sheldrake, *Entangled Life*, 82.

178 *to the fact that shared mycorrhizal networks*: Sheldrake, *Entangled Life*, 156.

179 *an abominable mystery*: Richard Buggs, "Darwin's Abominable mystery," *Ecology & Evolution*, May 24, 2017, ecoevocommunity. nature.com/posts/16792-darwin-s-abominable-mystery.

11. THE MOUNTING SAP

182 *And then there's Badger, of course*: Kenneth Grahame, *The Wind in the Willows* (New York: Henry Holt and Company, 1980), 7.

182 *simplicity among these fields*: Hinton, *Mountain Home*, 9.

183 *dynamic cosmology*: Hinton, *Mountain Home*, xiii.

183 *occurrence appearing of itself*: Hinton, *Mountain Home*, 279.

183 *Each day is a journey*: Bashō, *Backroads to Far Towns, Basho's OKU-NO-HOSOMICHI*, Cid Corman and Kamaike Susumu (trans.), (New York: Grossman, 1971), 15.

183 *Peter Matthiessen, author, naturalist*: Part of the passage from Carl Jung that made Peter Matthiessen jump out of his chair when he first read it: "The undiscovered vein within us is a living part of the psyche; classical Chinese philosophy names this interior way 'Tao,' and likens it to a flow of water that moves irresistibly towards its goal. To rest in Tao means fulfillment, wholeness, one's destination reached, one's mission done; the beginning, end, and perfect realization of the meaning of existence innate in all things." Peter Matthiessen, *The Snow Leopard* (New York: Penguin Group, 1978), 42.

184 *The search may begin with a restless feeling*: Matthiessen, *The Snow Leopard*, 41.

184 *as a boundless generative organism*: Hinton, *Mountain Home*, xv.

184 *The seeds are coming*: Rowen White, "Seed Rematriation," Sierra Seeds, March 19, 2018, sierraseeds.org/seed-rematriation.

185 *creative, fertile, fierce, loving*: White, "Seed Rematriation."

185 *The seeds, my teachers*: Rowen White, "Rowen's Story," Sierra Seeds, October 19, 2022, sierraseeds.org/rowens-story.

185 *the responsibility of growing food*: Salmón, *Iwígara*, 16.

186 *For Indigenous people, land is at the foundation*: In his fascinating book *The Habit of Turning the World Upside Down*, Howard Mansfield zooms in on our Western concept of land ownership: "Navigability, utility, that's our property creed. Everything is owned; everything has its use." Howard Mansfield, *The Habit of Turning the World Upside Down* (Peterborough, New Hampshire: Bauhan Publishing, 2018), 56.
Contrast this with the well-known words spoken by Sealth, a Duwamish chief, in 1865: "How can you buy or sell the sky—the warmth of the land? The idea is strange to us. We do not own the freshness of the air or the sparkle of the water. How can you buy them from us?" Peter Matthiessen, *Indian Country* (New York: Viking Press, 1984), epigraph.

186 *food, water, medicine*: Simon Ortiz, "Indigenous Sustainability: Language, Community Wholeness, and Solidarity," in *Traditional Ecological Knowledge: Learning from Indigenous Practices for Environmental*

Sustainability, ed. Melissa K. Nelson and Daniel Shilling (Cambridge, UK: Cambridge University Press, 2018), 89.

186 *That the Tewa see all life*: Alfonsi Ortiz, "Origins: Through Tewa Eyes," *Stars Above, Earth Below: American Indians and Nature*, ed. Marsha C. Bol (Boulder, CO: Roberts Rinehart, 1998), 257.

186 *as a prayer embodied*: White, "Rowen's Story."

187 *Sierra Seeds seeks to reseed*: "About," Sierra Seeds, sierraseeds. org/about.

188 Haatse *[land]* . . . *is the instigator of language*: Ortiz, "Indigenous Sustainability," 91.

188 *shade tree of support*: "Indigenous Seed Keepers Network," Native American Food Sovereignty Alliance, nativefoodalliance.org/ our-programs-2/indigenous-seedkeepers-network.

189 *to restore a person to his own country*: *The Compact Oxford English Dictionary*, 2nd ed. (1991), s.v. "repatriation."

189 *It simply means back to Mother Earth*: "Indigenous Seed Keepers Network," Native American Food Sovereignty Alliance.

190 *each one a whole universe of sustenance*: Sierra Seeds (website), sierraseeds.org.

190 *We are still here*: Rowen White, "A Note from Rowen," Sierra Seeds, sierraseeds.org/community.

12. FILTERS OF THE EARTH

197 *the phenomenology of roundness*: Gaston Bachelard, *The Poetics of Space: The Classic Look at How We Experience Intimate Places* (Boston: Beacon Press, 1969), 232.

197 *sturdy web of intimacy*: Bachelard, *The Poetics of Space*, 100.

197 *For it is obvious that the image*: Bachelard, *The Poetics of Space*, 104.

197 *I become once more a man*: Bachelard, *The Poetics of Space*, 94.

198 *A nest . . . is a precarious thing*: Bachelard, *The Poetics of Space*, 102.

200 *These trees need to be archived*: Jim Robbins, *The Man Who Planted Trees: A Story of Lost Groves, the Science of Trees, and a Plan to Save the Planet* (New York: Spiegel & Grau, 2015), 84.

200 *eco-cleansing filter systems*: Archangel Ancient Tree Archive (website), ancienttreearchive.org.

201 *I must return to my chosen story*: Within this chapter, I reference two books with the same title (and I recommend both). *The Man Who Planted Trees* by the French writer Jean Giono also had alternate titles: *The Story of Elzéard Bouffier, The Man Who Planted*

Hope and Reaped Happiness, and *The Most Extraordinary Character I Ever Met.* Unlike Elzéard Bouffier, David Milarch is very much a real person. Please visit ancienttreearchive.org.

202 *We're here to help Ireland:* Robbins, *The Man Who Planted Trees,* 147.

202 *These substances are at the heart:* Robbins, *The Man Who Planted Trees,* 59.

202 *the genetic information of a mother tree:* Beresford-Kroeger, *To Speak for the Trees,* 270.

205 *we place ourselves at the origin of confidence:* Bachelard, *The Poetics of Space,* 103.

EPILOGUE: A FLASH OF BEAUTY

208 *Wheel of Life:* Berry, *The Collected Poems of Wendell Berry, 1957–1982,* 231.

209 *I don't know what nature is:* Anahid Nersessian, "The Escape Artist," *New York Review of Books,* October 7, 2021, nybooks. com/articles/2021/10/07/fernandopessoa-escape-artist.

210 *Trees are right at the heart:* Tudge, *The Tree,* 368.

210 *We observed with astonishment:* Wulf, *The Invention of Nature,* 74.

210 *Humboldt has discovered the idea:* Wulf, *The Invention of Nature,* 74.

210 *the perfect symbol:* Wulf, *The Invention of Nature,* 74.

211 *Beth Moon has worked to raise awareness:* Concerned about the fate of the baobab, Beth Moon traveled to Senegal, Madagascar, and South Africa to document this extraordinary tree. *Baobab* is a moving accompaniment to her previous book, *Ancient Trees: Portraits of Time.*

211 *the sense of origins, of innocence and mystery:* Peter Matthiessen, Eliot Porter, *The Tree Where Man Was Born: The African Experience* (New York: E.P. Dutton & Co., 1972), author's note.

212 *our need to understand:* Matthiessen, *The Tree Where Man Was Born,* 232.

212 *Humans exist somewhere between the mountain:* Linda Hogan, "The Radiant Life with Animals," in *Traditional Ecological Knowledge: Learning from Indigenous Practices for Environmental Sustainability,* ed. Melissa K. Nelson and Daniel Shilling (Cambridge, UK: Cambridge University Press, 2018), 194.

212 *a way of relating respectfully:* Dennis Martinez, "Redefining Sustainability through Kincentric Ecology: Reclaiming Indigenous Lands, Knowledge, and Ethics," in *Traditional Ecological Knowledge: Learning from Indigenous Practices for Environmental*

Sustainability, ed. Melissa K. Nelson and Daniel Shilling
(Cambridge, UK: Cambridge University Press, 2018), 140.

212 *beauty, beautiful—a Navajo (or Dineh):* Joy Harjo, *A Map to the Next
World: Poetry and Tales* (New York: W. W. Norton & Company,
2000), 137.

213 *No word exists alone*: Leslie Marmon Silko, *Ceremony*, (New York:
Penguin Books, 1986), 35.

ADDITIONAL READING:

Anna Akhmatova, Roberta Reeder (ed.), Judith Hemschemeyer
(trans.), *The Complete Poems of Anna Akhmatova*

Eugenia Bone, *Mycophilia: Revelations from the Weird World of Mushrooms*

C. P. Cavafy, Rae Dalven (trans.), *The Complete Poems of Cavafy*

Guy Davenport, *Every Force Evolves a Form: Twenty Essays*

Brian Doyle, *One Long River of Song: Notes on Wonder*

Ernest Fenollosa, Ezra Pound (ed.), *The Chinese Written Character as a
Medium for Poetry*

Sir James George Frazer, *The Golden Bough*

Fred Hageneder, *The Meaning of Trees: Botany, History, Healing, Lore*

Olavi Huikari, *The Miracle of Trees*

Milton Kessler, *Free Concert: New and Selected Poems*

William Logan, *Oak: The Fame Civilization*

Barry Lopez and Debra Gwartney (eds.), *Home Ground: A Guide to the
American Landscape*

Joan Maloof, *Among the Ancients: Adventures in the Eastern Old-Growth
Forests*

Osip Mandelstam, James Greene (trans.), *Osip Mandelstam: Poems*

Lorine Niedecker, *T & G: The Collected Poems (1936–1966)*

Fernando Pessoa, James Greene, and Clara de Azevedo Mafra
(trans.), *The Surprise of Being: Twenty-Five Poems*

David Quammen, *The Reluctant Mr. Darwin : An Intimate Portrait of
Charles Darwin and the Making of His Theory of Evolution*

Gary Snyder, *The Old Ways*

Rebecca Solnit, *Orwell's Roses*

Frank Waters, *Masked Gods: Navaho & Pueblo Ceremonialism*

Terry Tempest Williams, *The Hour of Land: A Personal Topography of
America's National Parks*

Diane Wilson, *The Seed Keeper: A Novel*

C. D. Wright, *Casting Deep Shade: An Amble Inscribed to Beech Trees & Co.*

ACKNOWLEDGMENTS

Just as no word exists alone no book exists without the collaboration of many people and a circle of connectivity. First, I am grateful to Paul Bresnick, my agent and long-time friend, for suggesting another book, and for finding Milkweed Editions as publisher. Beyond the confines of my study, my books have found a place in the world, however modest that is, because of Paul: thank you.

I remember my first stimulating conversation with Daniel Slager, CEO of Milkweed Editions—the first of many I trust—and I am grateful for the partnership. And to those at Milkweed Editions who helped to shepherd the book into existence, thank you: Broc Rossell, Lauren Langston Klein, Mary Austin Speaker, Joanna Demkiewicz, Morgan LaRocca, Anna Thorsen, and Shannon Blackmer. And a heartfelt hug to Helen Whybrow, a true shepherd who lives in Vermont. By an auspicious twist of fate she became my editor for this book: "reciprocal alchemy" at work. Here's to celebrating twenty-five years of friendship and collaboration in support of the land we love, the words we cultivate. I extend that hug to my dear friend Peter Forbes at your shared brave little farm above the Mad River Valley.

I want to thank those who have continued the experiment at Quail Hill Farm following my "graduation" after thirty years: Layton Guenther, Brendan McMullen, Madison Aldrich, and all the apprentices who continue to turn up every year, full of passion and stamina. I treasure a friendship-of-the-soil with Paul Hamilton—one that has nourished the two of us for three decades. Michael Light, Deborah's son, has been a brilliant friend, and though the West captured him long ago, I welcome his return to this vibrant Eastern peninsula. With John de Cuevas I shared a love for birds, words, and garlic; he has passed on, but his passion for the land of Amagansett lives on through his daughter Maggie and her dear family..For the love and attention and frisky midwestern humor he has gifted to the land and to the broader community, we are thankful to Nick Stevens.

Thank you once again to John Halsey, founder and president of the Peconic Land Trust for four decades of creative conservation work. To John, Pam Greene, Yvette DeBow-Salsedo, and the board of PLT, I am grateful for the sabbatical that allowed me to travel throughout Europe in the autumn of 2018. Several members of the PLT board have supported my spade work and writing work for years, and I am deeply grateful for their recognition and friendship, especially: Tom Williams, Nancy Goell, Nancy Gilbert, Peter Talty, Lloyd Zuckerberg, and Steve Jones. Thank you to Rebecca Chapman, for her kindness and for years of camaraderie.

A generous grant from the Joyce and Irving Goldman Family Foundation gave me the chance to travel to Cornwall (once again); to Thessaloníki, Greece; and to Switzerland, and to return with stories. Thank you especially to Katja Goldman and Ben Binswanger.

Thank you to Wildsam and *The East Hampton Star*, who originally published passages from chapters 9 and 12.

Andrew Lanyon's artful book about his father, *Peter Lanyon: 1918–1964*, is a treasure, and I treasure a certain timeless decade in Penwith, raising children, and imagining. To my friends in Cornwall, I celebrate here our time together there: Liz and Tim Le Grice, Claire Lucas and family, Guy Royle and Debbie Prosser, Krysia Osostowicz and Simon Rowe, and my dear friend Peter Perry, a man of the trees if ever one was born.

Thank you to Jon Snow, redwood brother (!), and to the community of the Hayground School. It is a pleasure to continue to collaborate with our friends involved with Archangel Ancient Tree Archive: David Milarch, Cindy Spiegel, Kimi Green, Marianna Verlage Archibald, Jessica Hartsfield, Caryssa Rouser, and Jesse Ketchum. Becky Genia: your blessing of the young redwoods was a generous gift.

To my colleagues on the mountain trek toward the founding of the Peter Matthiessen Center, thank you, and may the alpine and sea breezes be favorable: Alex Matthiessen, Lillian Ball, Michael Haggiag, Lee Carlson, Paul Rogers, Daniela Kronemeyer, John Halsey, Kim Quarty, and so many supporters of the extraordinary life and work of Peter Matthiessen, Muryo Roshi. I bow to Maria Matthiessen, and to Rue Matthiessen; and I express gratitude to Michel (Engu) Dobbs, whose life quietly serves to remind us that every step of the way is the way.

Much gratitude to those whose words or work have influenced one chapter or another: Rowen White, Sarah Montgomery, Shi Yan, Jean Giblette, Paula Kessler, Michael Lynch, Tucker Marder, Mica Marder, Shane Weeks, Holger Winenga and Carrie Rebora Barratt of LongHouse Reserve, Sir Tim Smit, so welcoming and generous with his time. For years of tutelage, shared travel, and friendship, and for her excellent reporting (*The Prying Mantis*) to Elizabeth Henderson—thank you! And thank you to Edith Seligson for including my family as part of her family.

What a gift to camp out beside the Pecos River, home of Jeanette Hart-Mann and family, with the students fortunate to be enrolled in the Land Arts program at the University of New Mexico. Thank you to Jeanette and Bill, seed stewards extraordinaire, for the warm welcome. Thank you for shelter and laughter to our friends in Corrales, Geevy and Nancy Manierre, and to Kirsten Falke-Boyd for her appreciation of the bosque that borders the Rio Grande, and for our shared love of the lyrics of Seamus Heaney.

Gratitude to Gary Paul Nabhan and Laura Smith Monti (*Laurus nobilis*) for the foresight to imagine and arrange the seed summit held at Oak Spring Garden in Virginia in 2019; also to the passionate seed folks who attended, and to Sir Peter Crane for hosting the gathering.

I am full of praise for the work of Urgenci, The International Network for Community Supported Agriculture, guided with agility and finesse by general secretary Jocelyn Parot, working with producers and consumers for many years to promote agroecology, food sovereignty, and solidarity-economy policies worldwide.

I am thankful to Petra Page-Mann for her spirited work in communion with plants and seeds, and also for supplying the title for this book—I found it in her review of my previous book, *Seedtime*. For the gift of a lovely, expressive word, *psithurism*, thank you to Keith Douglas.

Should this book by chance find you, Bill and Shyla,

know that I am ever grateful for our formative time together, in Maine, decades ago, present still.

As a respite from the computer screen or the stacks of books to left and right I look above and to the altar of my desk: a copper Buddha by Bill King; a set of brass scales (a gift of Ivy Ermert); a gorgeous abstract painting by Liam; a painting of Bacchus (from the sculpture in the Jardin du Luxembourg, Paris) by Elaine de Kooning; a photo of my mother and father, early on, reflective, engaged with each other; and a cast aluminum sculpture of Napoleon by Bill King entitled *Decisions, Decisions*, a scroll of plans at his feet.

I commissioned my daughter, Rowenna, then age nine, to design and draw a series of cards; one card maintains a place on my desk, inspiration for this book. On the front page, an attractive pencil, sheets of paper with sparkles, the words, "To the cat A I dog words They," and on the back page, "Writers have to write." I am grateful for Row's instruction now, even as then.

Liam! Thank you once again (and again?) for the images, and for sharing your art. To Levin and Alexis— smack-dab in the midst of the challenging-stimulating-fantastic episode of raising a family—thank you for the gift of grandchildren. And to Megan, my dearest, in the words of Bashō: "Moon & Sun are passing figures of countless generations, and years coming or going wanderers too." We are wanderers who have found a home with each other, and with the gifts that germinate each day, beginning with the word. Last night a tidal thunder / cleansed the oaks. / As sound broke / the sleep of heartwood / I woke to find you here, / only a limb away.

Lindsay Morris

SCOTT CHASKEY is a poet, farmer, and educator. For thirty years he cultivated soil and community for the Peconic Land Trust at Quail Hill Farm in Amagansett, New York. A pioneer of the Community Supported Agriculture movement, he is past president of the Northeast Organic Farming Association of New York and was honored as Farmer of the Year in 2013. He was a founding board member for The Center for Whole Communities in Vermont and for Sylvester Manor Educational Farm in Shelter Island, New York, and he currently serves on the board for the Peter Matthiessen Center in Sagaponack, New York. He is the author of *This Common Ground: Seasons on an Organic Farm*, and *Seedtime: On the History, Husbandry, Politics, and Promise of Seeds*. With his wife, Megan, a musician and poet, he lives in the home in which they raised three children, in Sag Harbor, New York.

milkweed
EDITIONS

Founded as a nonprofit organization in 1980, Milkweed Editions is an independent publisher. Our mission is to identify, nurture, and publish transformative literature, and build an engaged community around it.

Milkweed Editions is based in Bdé Óta Othúŋwe (Minneapolis) within Mní Sota Makhóčhe, the traditional homeland of the Dakhóta people. Residing here since time immemorial, Dakhóta people still call Mní Sota Makhóčhe home, with four federally recognized Dakhóta nations and many more Dakhóta people residing in what is now the state of Minnesota. Due to continued legacies of colonization, genocide, and forced removal, generations of Dakhóta people remain disenfranchised from their traditional homeland. Presently, Mní Sota Makhóčhe has become a refuge and home for many Indigenous nations and peoples, including seven federally recognized Ojibwe nations. We humbly encourage our readers to reflect upon the historical legacies held in the lands they occupy.

milkweed.org

Milkweed Editions, an independent nonprofit publisher, gratefully acknowledges sustaining support from our Board of Directors; the Alan B. Slifka Foundation and its president, Riva Ariella Ritvo-Slifka; the Amazon Literary Partnership; the Ballard Spahr Foundation; *Copper Nickel*; the McKnight Foundation; the National Endowment for the Arts; the National Poetry Series; and other generous contributions from foundations, corporations, and individuals. Also, this activity is made possible by the voters of Minnesota through a Minnesota State Arts Board Operating Support grant, thanks to a legislative appropriation from the arts and cultural heritage fund. For a full listing of Milkweed Editions supporters, please visit milkweed.org.

Interior design by Tijqua Daiker and Mary Austin Speaker
Typeset in Baskerville

Baskerville is the most well-known of the typefaces designed in the 18th century by British printer, type designer and papermaker John Baskerville, who was also known to cut gravestones. A transitional typeface bridging the conventions of Old Style and Modern type, Baskerville was used to print John Milton's *Paradise Lost* in 1758, the *Holy Bible* in 1763, and the 1776 translation of *The Works of Virgil* into English.